Paddle-Wheel Days

IN CALIFORNIA

The Propeller Club
Port of the Golden Gate

This book is awarded to

Capt. Kenneth M. Graham

as an acknowledgement of his many years of service and contributions to the American Merchant Marine and allied industries, on this 26th day of November, in the year Nineteen-hundred, sixty-nine,

Paddle-Wheel

Days

IN CALIFORNIA

By

JERRY MacMULLEN

Illustrated by the Author

STANFORD UNIVERSITY PRESS
Stanford, California

The Propeller Club
Port of the Golden Gate

This book is awarded
to

Capt. Kenneth M. Graham

as an acknowledgement of
his many years of service
and contributions to the
American Merchant Marine
and allied industries, on
this 26th day of November,
in the year Nineteen-
hundred, sixty-nine,

Paddle-Wheel

Days

IN CALIFORNIA

By

JERRY MacMULLEN

Illustrated by the Author

STANFORD UNIVERSITY PRESS
Stanford, California

STANFORD UNIVERSITY PRESS, STANFORD, CALIFORNIA

Library of Congress Catalog Card Number: A44-4831
Printed in the United States of America
First published, 1944
Sixth printing, 1960

TO THE MEN OF THE RIVERS

It was their skill, attention to duty—and sense
of humor—that made travel safe and pleasant
in those grand old packets which, in happier
future times, perhaps will return to the
waters of the Golden State

FOREWORD

THE STORY of the sailing vessels that transported cargo coastwise in Spanish California, as well as offshore to Hawaii, South America, and the Atlantic seaboard, has been fully detailed and dramatized in the memoirs of Alfred Robinson, in those of William Heath Davis, and in that superb classic of the sea, Richard Henry Dana's *Two Years Before the Mast*. But until now no writer has brought together in one coherent account the history of steam river and bay craft or that of coastwise steamer traffic in California. There is little consideration of the latter herein; but it deserves, and no doubt ultimately will have, full-length book treatment.

The previous absence of collected information on inland-waterway transportation is largely responsible for widespread ignorance of the subject, even among California scholars. Few Californians realize, for instance, that at one time or another there was regular steamer service from Red Bluff, far up on the Sacramento, and from Watson's Landing, on the San Joaquin not far from Fresno, to San Francisco, and that this service continued until after the turn of the century.

Whereas sail was a concomitant of the pastoral days of pre-conquest California, steam came in with the Gold Rush to serve faithfully for nearly a century. Indeed, had it not been for inland steamers the production of gold from the mines of the Mother Lode, the Northern Diggin's, and the Trinity River would have been seriously impaired, and the subsequent agricultural development in the great valleys would have been long retarded.

Ironically, what the river steamers created in due course destroyed their usefulness. The cultivation of increasingly extended areas of land and the advent of irrigation severely drained the Sacramento and San Joaquin rivers. This circumstance, together with the extension of the railroads and the coming of highway transportation, inexorably put an end to the river craft.

There is a vast deal of important historical data in this book. There is even more of fascinating and romantic lore, about the rivers, about the steamers themselves, about the river men—and they were *men* in those days—and about the landings and other places the names of many of which have long since vanished from our maps.

Jerry MacMullen is not a professional historian. He is a competent newspaperman, at this writing serving ably in the United States Navy, who has long had a zealot's interest in watercraft and a particular passion for California steamers. Within these covers, with a high degree of literary felicity and an unswerving fidelity to historical fact, he recites a long-neglected chapter in California's annals.

PHIL TOWNSEND HANNA

September 1, 1944

PREFACE

THERE ARE SOME who feel that no historical work should be undertaken until all of those directly connected with the subject are dead. This may lead to a colder and more objective approach to the matter, but it also leads to missing a lot of fun. And it is the most certain means of eliminating intimate details of the everyday life of those who made the history which is under discussion.

In *Paddle-Wheel Days in California,* some pains have been taken to preserve as much of the fun and as many intimate details as possible. On the other hand, no pains whatever have been taken to produce a solemn and dignified work on inland navigation. Footnotes have been used largely to twit the text, and you will look in vain among them for *Ibid.,* that best-known authority on any subject.

Sources have been nothing if not varied—old newspaper files, steamship timetables, government publications, a job lot of histories, and the word-of-mouth legends passed, through thick tobacco smoke, in the cabins and pilothouses of the last of the California river packets. Wherever possible, material has been checked for corroboration from other sources. Much has been discarded; for instance, in the list of California river steamers, no names have been included which could not be found in official government publications or in contemporary newspaper advertisements or timetables.

Probably the most valuable single source was the file of the *Daily Alta California,* whose articles on shipping obviously were written by men who knew their subject. Another gold mine is a mimeographed publication of the United States Department of Commerce, *Steam Vessels Built in the United States, 1807–1856,* published in 1931. And the value of the *List of Merchant Vessels of the United States,* under its varying names and format from 1868 down through the years, is too obvious to need comment.

The work of compiling this material has been going on for several years, a great deal of it during a tour of duty in San Francisco which made the Bancroft Library of the University of California, the California Historical Society collection, and the pioneer department of the Wells Fargo Bank available during off-duty hours. To these organizations grateful acknowledgment is made; it is made as well to the staff of the Southern Pacific Railway, whose members, especially the late Lindsay Campbell, were most kind.

It would be impossible to list all of those who helped on the job. Outstanding, however, were: Henry Rusk, John Pausback, and Otis Oldfield of San Francisco; Captain Enos F. Fouratt and Laurence E. Fish, Laurence E. Bulmore, F. G. Camp, and Thomas Kenney—the last four being engineers—of the Southern Pacific vessels; W. P. Dwyer and Captains William J. and William B. Atthowe, W. H. Stoffel, and Herbert Kunzelman of The River Lines; Captain John H. Urton of the Petaluma & Santa Rosa Railroad; Chief Boatswain J. C. McNairn, U.S.N.R.; Melvin C. Mayne of the *San Diego Union;* and Carl Christensen of Eureka.

It is likely that, in spite of everything, some errors have crept in; it is hoped that these will be excused as unavoidable and that the book will be accepted for what it is—a rambling effort to record, before it is too late, a colorful minor phase of the history of California.

J. MacM.

San Diego, California
August 5, 1944

CONTENTS

LIST OF ILLUSTRATIONS

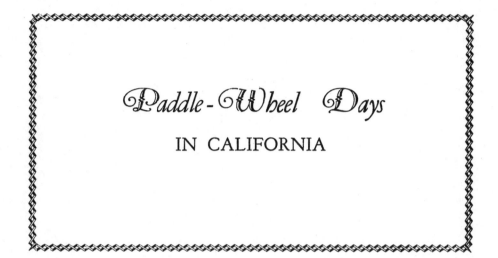

Paddle-Wheel Days

IN CALIFORNIA

Chapter I

A SHIP CAME IN FROM RUSSIA

THE LITTLE RUSSIAN CHURCH at Fort Ross was in somewhat better repair than it is today when the bark *Naslednich* climbed over the northwestern horizon and stood down the coast toward the Farallones. Not that there is anything unusual in this, for only a quarter of a century had passed since the Muscovites had hewn the church, with its adjoining blockhouse and stockade, out of the forest redwoods of Northern California. The next day the *Naslednich* turned east, clewed up her courses, backed her main topsail, and let go her ponderous, wooden-stocked anchor in the then clean waters of San Francisco Bay.

Of the Russian bark we know but little, unfortunately, her arrival on that summer day in 1847 having been of more than passing importance. It probably is safe, however, to picture her as an apple-bowed packet with a galleried stern, an atrocious steeve to her bowsprit, and hemp rigging which had a bad habit of going slack in warm weather. In all likelihood, she was none too tidy. But, be that as it may, she carried out her lawful business, which was to

discharge for the merchants of the sleepy little village and its hinterlands an assortment of gewgaws and raw materials always
loosely referred to as general cargo.

During her labors she brought forth, among other items, a
steamboat. It was a wretched little thing by modern standards,
being only thirty-seven feet long, and it was all in pieces; it had
been in use in Alaska and was named the *Sitka*.[1] Workmen lugged
the pieces ashore at Yerba Buena Island and turned to on the job
of assembly, under the guidance of a dour Russian. In due time the
Naslednich catted her anchor, sweated up her creaking topsail
yards, and stood out through the harbor's mouth, at that period
unmarred by bridgework. What became of her after that is not a
matter of record; for our purposes, her delivery of that physically
insignificant but historically important steamboat warrants these
few paragraphs.

The *Sitka* was consigned to one of the early merchants, William
A. Leidesdorff,[2] who ran her up and down the Bay for a while to
see if she really would work. Finally, on November 29, 1847, she
headed for the Sacramento River, reaching New Helvetia,[3] the
capital of Sutter's empire, in the somewhat unsatisfactory time of
six days and seven hours. The *Daily Alta California,* never a
journal to pull its punches, later reported that on the down-river
trip the *Sitka* was beaten into Benicia by an oxteam, to the tune of
four days. No, she was no flash packet, in any sense of the word.
Her engine was feeble and noisy; her hull was a mere nine feet
wide by a little more than three feet deep, and if a man stood on
her port guardrail he lifted her starboard paddle wheel out of the
water.

On February 12, 1848, a whooping "norther" came down across
San Francisco Bay and sank her. In time she was raised; her engines were taken out and wiped dry, to be used later in a small fac-

---

[1] Some historians call her the *Little Sitka,* which may or may not be correct.

[2] After whom is named Leidesdorff Street—a narrow byway which sneaks out
from behind a bank, dashes furtively across California Street, and plunges out of
sight between two skyscrapers of Steamship Row.

[3] Nothing is left of New Helvetia but the Helvetia Cemetery, whose permanent
guests include many who left this vale of tears as a result of steamboat explosions.

tory on shore, and she ended her days as the schooner *Rainbow*. May her memory linger—for it was she who introduced steam navigation to California's inland waterways. She opened an era which was to see "great steamers, white and gold" plying the Sacramento and San Joaquin rivers, more modest ones bearing the commerce of the smaller tributaries, and, far to the south, stern-wheelers plowing the Colorado's waters across the blazing desert with breech-clouted Cocopah Indians as deck hands.

A century spans the history of steamboating in California, with the possible exception of a few surviving ferries around San Francisco, and a lone stern-wheeler each on Petaluma Creek and Humboldt Bay. With five years of that century still to go there was left, in active service, only one stern-wheel freighter in all the length and breadth of California. Progress—if you care to call it that—finished the steamboats and their colorful history which reached its peak in Bonanza days. Railway competition, truck competition, labor squabbles—all played their part. On California's rivers the subdued chunking of paddle wheels and the pipe-organ notes of the steam whistle have given way to the blat of the compressed-air horn and the annoying "boom-boom-boom-boom" of Herr Doktor Diesel's highly efficient (but unromantic and smelly) invention.

California's steamboat trade was born of the Gold Rush; had not James Marshall detected the gleam of yellow metal in the mill-race on the fateful afternoon of January 19, 1848, it is likely that the little *Sitka* would have had a much smaller following in the years which followed. California mushroomed in population and prices;[4] San Francisco was some distance away from the diggings, and there were no roads worthy of the name. The splendid system of natural waterways was the answer, and while it was the stagecoach or the oxcart which got the miner to his ultimate destination, it was the river steamboat which carried him on the first—and perhaps most important—leg of the journey. San Francisco, in those

---

[4] A lot on Montgomery Street, near Washington, sold in July 1848 for $10,000; in November the same lot, with a small shanty on it, brought $27,000. Flour was two dollars a pound, coffee and sugar were twice that, and a bottle of whisky cost twenty dollars.

days a squalid settlement of tents and shacks, was all but deserted in May 1849, everyone having gone out in search of gold. And most of them went by some form of river transportation. That symbol of the old West, the Pony Express, also was tied in with the early steamboats; many a letter posted in the East was transferred from a sweaty saddlebag to a purser's safe in a river boat, for final delivery in San Francisco.

In her palmy days, the river boat was a side-wheeler of rather ornate design; and this style of naval architecture, which was introduced by the steamers from the Atlantic States, continued on for years. River boats were graceful craft, their lean hulls capable of an excellent turn of speed. In the forward end of the hull was the "China hold" for Oriental passengers; then came the machinery space, which extended up through the entire structure; and aft, in some cases, was the dining room. On the main deck they stowed cargo, and there also were the offices and some of the staterooms. Topside was another deckhouse or cabin, its main feature being the "social hall"; and then came the uppermost weather deck, marked by the monitor roof of the main cabin, the gallows frame of the walking beam, and the "texas," where the officers—and the ultra-ultra passengers—were accommodated. The pilothouse was forward of the texas, or on top of it.

In the later stern-wheelers, the hold was too shallow to be of much use, aside from its rather important function of keeping the whole business afloat. It accommodated boilers, tanks, and part of the machinery. The main deck generally was devoted to cargo space and the rest of the engines, with the main cabin, the staterooms, and other passenger facilities above that. Staterooms were plain but comfortable, dining rooms were well appointed, and the cooking was above reproach.

The dyed-in-the-wool Californian is choosy about his food; a mediocre table is all well enough for some, but he demands—and on the river boats he got—the best and plenty of it. That steady run of multi-course dinners probably would have wrecked any but a stout digestive system, and how the steamers' own people stood up under it is a mystery. Probably ample exercise was the answer.

Fresh game and fish, oversized oysters, roasts and local vegetables, paunch-producing pastries, and strong coffee—to say nothing of a garish assortment of pickles, preserves, and sauces and of beverages ranging from champagne to Dago Red—were the accepted thing on the river in those dear, dead days. A nostalgic description has been handed down by an old-time bartender from the famous *New World*: "You et all the way from Rye-oh Visty to San Francisco, and only a dollar. Ah—what a meal! What a meal!"

It was an era of expansion, in other things as well as in meals. The steamboats, by increasing in size and in number, merely were keeping pace with the times. And in their development on the California streams we see an interesting blend of the types of the Hudson and other Eastern streams with those of the Mississippi and the Ohio. From this union there emerged the Western river steamboat, and with her perfection there developed, as well, an important industry which lasted for the better part of a century. In its later years, it provided transportation for passengers and for thousands of tons of fresh and processed foodstuffs from the farms to the big refrigerator steamships which hauled them to the far corners of the world. Up river, they carried building materials, fuel, farm implements, and mining equipment — everything needed to satisfy the appetite of an expanding state.

By day and by night those steamers made the run from the broad expanse of San Francisco Bay, through narrow Carquinez, and on past the myriad islands of the Delta country to where the rivers wind away from the sea, back toward the distant hills. Dazzling summer sun picked out their white paintwork and silhouetted them, cameo-clear, against the willows and cottonwoods which line the banks, the varying shades of green accented by dark blobs of mistletoe clinging to the branches above the slowly moving stream. Then cabin and pilot-house windows were dropped, giving to crews and passengers the luxury of a breeze as they watched the heat waves shimmering above the broad, yellow stretches of valley land. Later would come the rains of winter, when the steamers struggled valiantly against the surge of high water from mountains and canyons sweeping irresistibly on to the sea. And there were days and nights of fog—a foggy night with a full moon was the worst—when the pilots had to guess just when they were opposite the cottonwood with a branch broken off on its west side that lined up with a little ruined adobe house at the precise moment for giving her three spokes of the wheel for the next turn.

Prospectors, Chinamen, empire-builders, gunmen, tinhorns, and trollops; rural blades bound for the delights of the City, Kanakas, bindle stiffs, merchants, bankers, and Filipino farmhands; turbaned Hindus on their way to the rice fields—their passenger lists were nothing if not cosmopolitan. Operating them were dignified masters and pilots, portly engineers—who in bygone days avoided a too-close scrutiny of their steam gauges if there was a rival to be beaten—roustabout deckhands, and softly padding Chinese stewards. And there was the bartender, with his suave manner and handlebar moustache; he, sir, was a gentleman—and if you questioned it, he could clear the bar with one leap and play the "Anvil Chorus" on you with a bung starter. Gone are the red-shirted miner, the empire-builder, and the soft-spoken gentleman in the ruffled shirt and Prince Albert who generally had a deadly Derringer tucked in the waistband of his pantaloons.

Into the lusty days of their youth those boats crowded adventure, tragedy, cut-throat competition, racing, disaster—and the off-the-record romances of more than one Bay region Lothario. With their growing pains out of the way, the river boats provided dependable transportation at attractive rates, both for business purposes and for the relaxation of the jaded and weary.

They catered to an age when people had time to live—time to stand in the lee of the texas on a sparkling winter night and watch the stars, so bright that they seemed to rest just above the murky skeleton of the hogging frame and the crown of the tall smokestack, and there was no sound but the soft chunking of paddle wheels and the subdued "Ssooo, haah! Ssooo, haah!" of a slow-speed steam engine. And it was remarkable how even that slight sound would carry across the water on a still night, punctuated by the rising and falling cadence of the buckets—faster as the long, gleaming piston approached the fullness of its stroke, slower as it crossed center; you could count the engine revolutions by listening for that slight variation in the rhythm of the wheels. And there were nights when the moon would come, huge and golden, up from behind the distant mountains, lighting up the fields and throwing inky-black shadows from the trees along the banks—a twinkling light in a farmhouse window, level with the deck on which you stood; cattle standing motionless in the fields; the low squawk of some night bird—

The inland liner is gone, probably for all time. Along the river's bank a metaled road carries the commerce which formerly went by boat; overhead the skies reverberate with the roar of air-craft bearing those to whom time is money and who probably could transact their business just as well with a three-cent stamp. People have forgotten the *Sitka,* the *Chrysopolis,* and the rest. With the passage of time we have achieved that which, for one reason or another, we term advancement.

Chapter II

AROUND THE HORN

Startled San Franciscans who have rubbed their eyes at the spectacle of a former New York "L" train scuttling out to Richmond with a load of tin-hatted shipyard workers should stop and consider the fact there there is nothing new under the sun. The westward migration of industry during World War II, with its resultant load on Western transportation facilities, is merely repetition of what occurred—if possible, in an even more bizarre manner—in the years immediately following the discovery of the gold which became such a headache to Johann Sutter.

Kipling has observed that you can get men who will cross the North Atlantic in winter on a pile-driver under tow, if the pay is good and the food even passable. And a veteran West Coast steam-schooner master once sourly observed: "Annybotty vot goes to sea, for Crice sake, iss cracy!" So, when transportation facilities for the land out beyond the prairies and mountains were sorely needed, there were stalwart souls who could be prevailed upon to take river steamers down around South America and on—the hard way—to the Golden Gate. As a result, many a side-wheeler which ended her days on the California rivers had to her credit the long voyage around through the Straits of Magellan. Staggering under as much fuel as they could carry, one after another would steam out from New York or Boston, touch perhaps at a few ports below the Mason and Dixon's line and in the West Indies, on down to Rio and other sources of coal—or wood—in South America, and finally plunge into the bleak passage from which they emerged, leaving the snow-capped mountains astern, to brave the winds of the Pacific and begin clawing their way north. Oddly enough, most of them made it in good enough condition to be of some future use. The answer probably is that, in those days, all vessels were built to take it.

The smaller ones were, of course, barred from this madcap adventure by their low fuel capacity—but that did not halt their participation in the California trade. Engines were dismantled and smeared with grease, hulls too large to go as a deckload were taken apart, and the whole business was loaded into a windjammer and sent on its way, to be put together on some beach around San Francisco Bay.[1]

Nearly two years passed after the *Sitka* made her first attempt at inland steam navigation in California and then decided to become a sailing vessel before anything other than wind-driven craft ventured on the California rivers. Then the first Eastern importation made its appearance—the *Lady Washington,* which, we are told, was "assembled" at Sutter's Embarcadero, and took the water on August 9, 1849. Already—on March 22—the *John A. Sutter* had been advertised for the San Francisco–Sutterville run, with her announced starting date some months farther along; but apparently she had failed to make her scheduled run. The *Lady Washington,* a flat-bottomed stern-wheeler, in due time chugged bravely up the Sacramento and American rivers to Coloma, started back, struck a snag, and went to the bottom. But she was raised, with the crude salvage equipment of the time, and lived to run again as the *Ohio.* She was the first steamboat to negotiate the waters of the American and her first voyage ties in rather definitely

---

[1] Hence the notation in various references, including government publications, that a vessel was "built in San Francisco" should be accepted with mental reservations.

with the Gold Rush, for she went to the very place where the precious and at times troublesome metal was discovered. Another craft, the *Pioneer,* was assembled at Benicia, also in August, for the river service. And the first advertised—and successful—steamboat schedule to Sacramento from San Francisco was that of the *Sacramento,* published and inaugurated in September. This steamer had been put together at Washington, across the river from Sacramento, for Captain John Van Pelt, and for some time she ran between the up-river metropolis and "New York of the Pacific"— the grandiose title of a small settlement on the south shores of Suisun Bay.

The famous *Senator,* built in New York in 1848 for the run between Boston and St. John, New Brunswick, left New York on March 10, 1849, and, reaching San Francisco on October 27, went almost immediately into service between that city and Sacramento. For many years she alternated between the river trade and the coastwise run to San Diego and way ports, reaching the end of the trail in 1882, when her engines were removed. Two years later, under sail, she went to New Zealand, and was converted into a coal hulk.

Meanwhile other paddle-wheels were churning salt water, as Eastern steamboats headed for the land where a ship could pay for herself in a few months' time.[2] Likewise in 1849 the opposition steamers, the *California* and the *Sarah,* competitors on the run between Haverhill and Newburyport, decided to become rivals in a big way and headed for California. At about the same time as the *Senator,* the Boston Steam Packet Line's *Commodore Preble,* the *General Warren,* and the Bangor Line's *W. J. Pease* got away from the Atlantic seaboard, with their windows shuttered, and fuel piled in wherever it could be stowed. The *W. J. Pease* got only as far as Montevideo; there her weary hull and strained boilers gave up, and she was condemned.

[2] The engine first intended for a dredge was set up in a small scow, which started running on the Feather River with the modest tariff of bricks at $1.00 each and lumber at a mere $150 a thousand feet; after two months of this high finance, the scow was auctioned off for $40,000.

The owners of the stern-wheeler *Governor Dana,* built for the upper Penobscot, found in the California trade a welcome escape from an embarrassing situation. It seems that, when the vessel was ready for use, someone discovered that another operator had been granted the exclusive use of the upper Penobscot, as far as steamboats were concerned. Irked but not dismayed by this situation, her owners calmly tore her to pieces, stuffed her into the hold of a sailing vessel, and shipped her to California. The *Hartford* got away from the Eastern seaboard at about the same time as the *Senator* squadron; but she must have encountered internal misery along the way, for it took her nearly a year to get to California.

The trim *Antelope,* a former Long Island Sound excursion steamer, answered the call of the Gold Rush and came West to take her place as a speedy favorite on the Sacramento, where she maintained a tight schedule with regularity. It fell to her lot to carry to San Francisco, on April 15, 1860, the first mail brought in, as far as Sacramento, by the Pony Express. Later she was a connecting link with Sonoma, via Petaluma Creek, and her employment in carrying gold dust and bullion for Wells Fargo's Express won her the nickname of "The Gold Boat." Another former deep-water steamer on the rivers during the early days was the iron steamboat *McKim,* a propeller-driven vessel of 400 tons. She arrived from New Orleans, where she had finished her job as an Army transport in the Mexican War, on October 3, 1849.

And there was, of course, the famous "stolen steamboat." It was mid-April of 1850 that the affairs of William H. Brown, a New Yorker, reached what might be termed a state of financial unrest if not an actual crisis. On the ways lay his pride and joy— the magnificent 530-ton side-wheeler *New World.* She was ready for launching; the red-plush upholstery and marble-topped tables in her cabins were the latest and best obtainable; her glittering brass chandeliers really dazzled the eye; and Brown regarded the world as a very lovely place indeed. Then came a solemn delegation to what should have been a festive affair. Certain of Brown's creditors, apparently feeling that all was not well, had attached the vessel. Humorless deputy sheriffs tacked on her pilothouse door

those soul-crushing documents which announce indebtedness, sei-
zure, confiscation, and/or sale at public auction on the courthouse
steps to protect the property rights of those who had supplied the
nails, the paint, and the oakum. The sheriff's goons seated themselves on the most comfortable sofas, and scratched matches on
the white enamel-work to light their stogies; they were prepared
for a lengthy visit, at so much a day, to be paid by the luckless
Brown after the *New World*'s bones had been picked by the legal
buzzards.

But Brown was a resourceful soul, as was Captain Ned Wakeman, his skipper. Surely, it would be all right to go on with the
launching? A vessel could be as firmly attached at a wharf as on
a launching-slip. Steam up? Why, yes, so it was; no doubt the
engineer had just fired up the boilers to keep them from rusting.
Think nothing of it, gentlemen! Nothing! Just an old steamboat
custom—

The *New World* shook herself slightly and moved down the
ways. Once in the water, her huge paddle wheels turned and, in
a widening sheet, creamy froth spread away from her slashing
buckets. As she headed down the harbor, the deputies demanded
an explanation from Captain Wakeman. The explanation which
they got had to do with the size and versatility of the captain's
doubled fist, and with the authority which is—or at least, which
in those days was—vested in the master of a steamer. Later in the
day the deputies, bellowing at this gross violation both of their own
civil liberties and of the orderly processes of law, were lowered
over the side in a pulling boat. Captain Wakeman kindly pointed
out to them the direction in which they might row if they did not
wish to be late for supper. With that he waved them a cheery
farewell—a gesture, no doubt, in which the fingers were aided
somewhat by the thumb and the nose. By dusk the *New World*
was hull down on the southern horizon.

That was April 13, 1850. Almost three months later she steamed
majestically in through the Golden Gate, not only having safely
negotiated the South American circuit but having, in some manner
which is not made quite clear, acquired three hundred cash cus-

tomers en route. With the prices which people were paying in those days for any kind of transportation to California, it is safe to assume that her first venture was anything but a financial flop. She took her place in California's transportation service on August 3, and for years afterward the graceful steamer, with her many-noted calliope and her bountiful table, was a favorite with travelers between San Francisco and the diggings. For a decade she plied the inland waters; then she sought new fields in the Puget Sound area and the Columbia River, from which she returned a few years later to run as a Vallejo ferry. She went to the wreckers in 1879—and may her memory remain green.

Another oddity in the transfer of tonnage from the Atlantic to the Pacific was the 120-foot stern-wheel steamboat *S. B. Wheeler,* built in faraway St. Stephens, New Brunswick, expressly for the California trade. As she was nearing completion, there stood on the stocks near by the open hull of the bark *Fanny.* In time the *Fanny* herself—sans deck—was launched. Then, those who were not in on the deal were scandalized to see the *Fanny*'s utterly mad builders take her out into fairly deep water and sink her. But it was all part of the plan; over her they floated the empty hull of the *S. B. Wheeler,* and then, in the manner of a floating drydock, they raised the *Fanny.* Of course, she caught the *Wheeler* on the way up. Now the steamboat's engines and upper works were stowed in the hold, the *Fanny* was decked and rigged, and not long afterward she clawed her way around the Horn. Arriving in San Francisco, she was sent directly to Benicia. There her yards were sent down, her masts and rigging removed, and her deck torn up. They sank her for a second time, and thus re-floated the *S. B. Wheeler!* The steamboat was towed to the fitting-out dock for her engines and upper works, and the marsupial *Fanny*—which by this time must have become reconciled to such monkey-business—was pumped out, re-rigged, and sent back to the sea lanes as an honest and God-fearing bark, with no more tricks up her sleeve. For some time the *S. B. Wheeler* plugged along between San Francisco and Stockton; then she was sold Mexican, and so far as available records are concerned her story ends.

All this time, others were exploring the upper reaches of the rivers. In the fall of 1849 the *Linda* started on the run between Sacramento and Yuba City, and in April 1850 the *Aetna* reached as far inland as Norristown, on the American. Early in May[8] of the same year the *Jack Hays* got to Redding, far up the Sacramento and only forty-three miles from the Trinity diggings. Late in 1851 Captain Albert Foster's larger *Orient* got nearly that far, making Red Bluff, and for some time, during high-water periods, continued to call at that town; when the water was low, she went only as far as Colusa.

An important figure in these early operations was Lieutenant James Blair, U.S.N. An associate of the Aspinwalls of New York and Philadelphia, he came to California at the height of the gold excitement and was the *Senator*'s pilot on her first trip up the river. But inland navigation was but an incident in his career; it was he who organized and built, at Rincon Point in San Francisco, the Sutter Iron Works. It was a plant erected solely for the purpose of setting up hulls and engines of steamboats which had been sent around, in knockdown form, from the East coast, and it was staffed entirely by the pick of Philadelphia's shipwrights and engineers. Blair remained at the head of the firm until his death in 1853.

And now had come the time of successful building, in California's yards, of her own steamboats. The youthful state was getting its feet on the ground, and, while the engines for her vessels still came, in most cases, from Eastern foundries, the forests of the Mendocino country were to produce the timber for the staunch hulls, the ornate and graceful cabins, and the fan-slatted boxing over the huge paddle wheels. No more would startled aborigines behold the former pride of the Hudson, the Penobscot, and Long Island Sound bravely fighting their way westward through the icy and wind-swept waters of Magellan.

[8] An interesting arrival that month, from the East, was a vessel appropriately named the *Gold Hunter;* she later was rebuilt as the schooner *Active,* of the United States Coast & Geodetic Survey.

An importation from the Atlantic seaboard, the *Senator* was the first deep-water vessel to visit Sacramento.

Sacramento water front in 1879, with the *Yosemite* at the landing

Express mail to San Francisco

Chapter III

DOG EAT DOG

COMPETITION is the life of trade. It is, moreover, sometimes the prelude to a lawsuit, an affair with pistols—and a coroner's inquest. Rugged individualism is a polite term for getting yours while the getting is good, and certain forms of piracy and strong-arm have with the passage of time become mellowed under the appellation "empire building."

It would be more pleasant—and less interesting—if history were to record that all the big steamboats and the little steamboats on California's inland waterways got together in the manner of one big, happy family. But such a history would be, to say the very least, a trifle fuzzy in its presentation of facts. When one considers the scores of vessels which were loose on the rivers and sloughs at that time, it is not strange that anything could happen. The only wonder is that it wasn't worse.

By the end of 1850, there were twenty-eight steamboats on the

17

Sacramento and Feather rivers alone; the same year, incidentally, saw twenty-three barks, nineteen brigs, and twenty-one brigantines arriving at Sacramento from the offshore routes. The bark *Whiton,* 241 tons, sailed up to Sacramento that year, with royal yards crossed, in seventy-two hours after a 140-day run from New York. How a square-rigger, even with a fair wind, made her way so quickly up the tortuous stream for better than a hundred miles is not explained; it must have been a feat of seamanship worth watching. Of course, at that time, the Sacramento was deeper than it is today, as the debris from hydraulic mining had not yet choked it; deep-sea windjammers—and even the *Senator,* with her draft of nine and one-half feet—couldn't have made it after the hydraulic people got busy.

With that steadily mushrooming fleet on the river, and with the chilling hand of the Steamboat Inspection Service not yet laid upon honest and God-fearing gamblers with the lives of the traveling public, steamboating on the Western streams became a knock-down, drag-out affair. A river captain, in many cases, owned his own vessel and ran it until it wore out, caught fire, rammed another or got rammed by it, blew up, or was snagged. With the shoestring independents, anything approaching a normal repair schedule was unheard of. Innocent of incorporation or of trade name, advertisements in the early papers were anonymous except for some such signature as "Joe Gish, Agent." Sometimes Joe owned the vessel outright; sometimes he was merely an individual hired by the owner-pilot because of his silvery tongue and the strong arms with which he corralled passengers from rival craft when oratory failed.

Along the San Francisco water front, these runners made the air ring with their advocacy of whatever asthmatic old pot paid them for their services. Each one represented ". . . . the finest steamer on the river—famous for her cuisine—just completely over-hauled and absolutely safe." This they bawled at the crowds of miners and adventurers just in from the East by clipper or by ox team, and they interlarded their praise with the most scurrilous descriptions of rival craft. Sometimes the opposing runners would become so sincere in their remarks that they would remove their coats and attempt to settle it with bare fists; not infrequently a prospective customer would have his arms all but wrenched from their sockets as rival runners would seize him and attempt to drag him in several directions at once.

With this veritable mob of steamboats loose upon the waters of the Sacramento, the San Joaquin, the American, and the Feather rivers—to say nothing of Alviso and Petaluma creeks—the days of overnight fortunes ended. Any lowering of the tariff by any one boat was immediately met—and beaten—by a dozen others. The rate of one dollar apiece for bricks and $30 per head for passengers went out the window, as did all ideas of caution and the inescapable axiom that if you overstrain machinery and hulls indefinitely you will pay heavily in the end. Fares to Sacramento tumbled to a dollar, to fifty cents, to a dime. Some super zealots sought good will by offering to carry passengers free, no doubt with the idea of making it up from the receipts of the bar. It was a wild, dizzy, hell-roaring period, marked by a carefree disregard of danger.

And still they came, a motley procession of side-wheelers around from the East Coast and others from California's own few yards. Littleton & Company launched the 120-ton *Shasta* at their Rincon Point yard in 1853—the first steamboat built on the West Coast. She was 110 feet long, with a beam of 23 feet and a depth of hold of 3½, and she drew 18 inches of water, which made her handy for the upper reaches of the rivers. She had two engines of 60 horsepower each and was the object of no small amount of "we point with pride" in her time. Had the wild Indians of California's early navigation kept up indefinitely, it is likely that dozens of other yards would have come up like mushrooms; but already the independent owners were beginning to feel the pinch of their own rate-cutting. The same year which saw the first steamboat completely built in California saw also the last one constructed for private account—the *Rip,* a 150-foot stern-wheeler, later renamed the *Pike,* and a steady performer of several years.

It was early in 1854 that the various owner-captains—and the more astute businessmen who had amassed several steamboats and several headaches—decided that collaboration rather than open warfare might prove beneficial. Wherefore, in March of that year, the shipping tycoons put on their collars and ties and sat down at a peace table, from which emerged the California Steam Navigation Company—a name which has been of some importance in California river history.

At the gathering was Charles Minturn, representing the big Sacramento steamers *Senator* and *New World,* and also the *Cornelia,* which ran up the San Joaquin as far as Stockton. Captain David Van Pelt, famous on the rivers, was there to see that no one stacked the cards against the dainty *Antelope.* The interests of the low-pressure steamers, the *Confidence,* the *Wilson G. Hunt,* and the *Thomas Hunt,* were guarded by Richard Chenery and R. M. Jessup; the high-pressure Stockton boats, *Helen Hensley* and *Kate Kearny,* were represented by a trio of river operators, Major S. J. Hensley, Captain James Whitney, Jr., and William Norris, who also contributed the *Hartford.* The Lubbock boys, Henry and Cap'n Bill, brought with them their title to the *American Eagle,* of the San Joaquin River, and an undersized packet named the *Sophie* was represented by one Louis McLane. Captain Thomas Lyle came down from the diggings and upheld the honor and dignity of the *John Bragdon,* the *Urilda,* and the *Camanche,*[1] which were able to get up as far as Marysville if the water in the river wasn't too low.

Chenery was elected president and things began to move. Soon General Alfred Redington's stern-wheelers, the *Gazelle,* the *Plumas,* the *Cleopatra,* and the *Gem,* and, from the river above Sacramento, the *Pike* (ex-*Rip*) and the *H. T. Clay* were brought into the fold. The total value of the Company's steamers was fixed at $1,250,000, and stock was sold at $1,000 a share. Included in the cumshaw was the proviso that anyone owning a modest $10,000 worth of stock could ride free. Unfortunately, these upper-bracket boys were not above a bit of chiseling on their fellow stockholders—a practice not unknown even in that era—and

---

[1] The Ohio River's contribution to winning the West, these three were built in Pennsylvania and shipped out, sectionally, in windjammers.

took to renting out their passes to hotel runners and others who had occasion to do a lot of river traveling. Soon the screams of the oppressed minority resulted in passes being discontinued—someone is always spoiling things.

One of the first things to do, of course, was to set a tariff which would enable the owners to recoup some of the losses incurred during the period in which they would not have sat down at a table together unless heavily armed and which at the same time would not encourage some smart aleck to start an opposition line. It was decided that those wishing to go to Marysville could afford to pay twelve dollars for so doing; two dollars less would get a passenger to Sacramento; and anyone who wanted to go to Stockton and didn't have eight dollars probably had no business in Stockton anyhow. This was, of course, the fare only; cabin, meals, liquor, and other necessities were charged up as extras. Freight was $6.00 a ton to Stockton, $8.00 to Sacramento, and $15 to Marysville. If you wanted to ship anything to Red Bluff, the head of navigation on the Sacramento system, you could enrich the line by $50 a ton or hire an oxcart and take it there yourself.

In the interests of dignity, a title of some sort apparently was a prerequisite to the portfolio of agent at a river port, for we find Governor F. F. Low as agent at Marysville, Captain James Johnson at Stockton, and Captain Lyle at Sacramento. The last named was replaced at an early date by General Redington.[2]

It was good service—but the public was fickle. Rural pundits, who had howled bloody murder at the unregulated racing which was good business for no one but the undertakers, now bent over their old Washington hand presses to denounce that favorite butt of the demagogue, monopoly. Up Marysville way it must have been pretty bad, for hardly had the new line got to running smoothly when the bearded leaders of that community decided that they had been wronged by the bigwigs from Sacramento, Stockton, and San Francisco and formed the Citizens' Steam Navigation Company of Marysville. It was no empty gesture, either. They knocked together a big high-pressure steamer called the

[2] Apparently the General ranked the Captain out of his job.

Queen City and put her on the river, at lower rates, in opposition
to the wicked combine. They followed this first thrust with the
sizable stern-wheeler *Young America*. As the merchants of Marysville were largely behind this opposition, and hence in a position to
put the heat on shippers and receivers of cargo, the competition
began to hurt. Dollar by dollar the prices came down; quart by
quart the demand for red ink went up. Finally both sides began
to weaken, and once more the peace-table scene was repeated.
The Marysville interests, realizing that they had at least a high
nuisance value, bargained sharply throughout, and in the end the
directors of California Steam dug grimly into the sock and paid the
upstarts to get them out of their hair. Up went the rates again.
Once more monopoly reared its ugly head, and the country editors
got back into their stride. Other "opposition" lines developed,
from time to time, but for the most part they were noted more for
their audacity than for their longevity.

In 1855, the year that the Marysville line folded up, Captain
Lyle brought the big high-pressure steamer *Eclipse* out from Cin-
cinnati for California Steam; the following year the *Surprise,* a
low-pressure steamer, arrived from New York. Later, with the
Thomas Hunt, the *Surprise* moved to the lusher fields of the Fraser
River, during the gold excitement there. The *Thomas Hunt* apparently remained in the north; but the *Surprise* came back briefly
to California, where later she was sold to Chinese interests.

The year 1860 saw the building of a vessel which was to be an
all-time darling of the rivermen—the almost legendary *Chrysopolis,* of which more anon. A year later an opponent bearing
the ominous name of Captain Kidd[3] entered the field, having acquired a large high-pressure steamboat named the *Nevada,* which
lasted for two years more and finally was wrecked while racing.
The famous low-pressure *Yosemite*—of grisly memory—was built
in 1863, to be followed a year later by another entry from Captain
Kidd, the *Washoe.* She, too, was destined to write her name in
letters of flame and scalding steam across the pages of river history.

[3] Whose venture will be discussed more fully in the succeeding chapter, which
deals with death by violence.

In 1866 the line built its last big steamer—the *Capital,* a 277-footer, which will be remembered as the biggest of the lot.

And now the railroads had come. Moreover, hydraulic mining had been introduced, and with no laws to stop them the backers of this form of enterprise had no care for others. The mud and debris from their mining operations rolled down into the rivers; the Sacramento became the muddy stream which it is today. All too clearly, the California Steam Navigation Company saw the handwriting on the wall. True, the steamboats were to last for many years, as feeders for the railroads and for handling cargo and passengers at cheap rates which the rails could not hope to meet—but the golden age of steamboating had ended. Wherefore, in 1871, they sold out to the California Pacific Railroad, for $620,000, and many of the "floating palaces" of those colorful days were converted into ferryboats, broken up, or hauled up on the river bank and left to rot.

Country editors who characterized the California Steam Navigation Company as a monopoly were certainly speaking within the bounds of fact. But this much should be borne in mind: it was unusual in that it was a monopoly of independents. One thing which made it go was the fact that the owners of many of the vessels worked aboard themselves or were intimately associated with the shore-side operations. When a steamboat owner gets out on the levee and pushes a hand-truck, then climbs aboard, puts on his peaked cap, and gives her one bell and a jingle for the trip down stream, he is something of a rugged individualist even if he is associated in a corporation with other owners.

During its life, the outfit is reported to have paid dividends which came to better than three hundred per cent. And when it was all washed up, the stockholders received, in cold cash, just about what their original stock had cost them. It had been, one might say, a very nice deal indeed.

CHAPTER IV

ONE SHOULD NOT TAKE LIBERTIES
WITH STEAM

BY PROVING THAT it was unnecessary to consume fourteen hours on the run between Sacramento and San Francisco, the *New World,* on April 2, 1851, opened the door to fast inland transportation. She also paved the way for some of the most gaudy and exhibitionistic funerals which California has ever seen. The *New World* did it, that spring day, in five hours and thirty-five minutes, and the idea seems to have taken hold at once. At any rate, the devil-may-care crews which made up the steamboat fraternity of the time immediately took to racing, both as a sporting proposition and to prove—if they could—that some one boat was better than any of the rest. Competition led to speed, and speed in many cases led to disaster. The fact that the *Fawn* had blown up on August 18, 1850, was no deterrent; the fifty dead of the *Sagamore* (she went sky-high on October 29 of the same year, just as she left the wharf for Stockton) already were forgotten, and the explosion of the *Major Tompkins* on January 23, 1851, should have taught its lesson, but it hadn't. Even the *New World,* shortly before, had killed seven with a ruptured steam-line while going through Steamboat Slough. And so, hundreds of men and women were to lose their lives by explosions within the next few years as a result of the craze for speed, to say nothing of those who drowned when the *Camanche* rammed the *John Bragdon* in Suisun Bay on January 3, 1853.

Some two years, in which the special Providence which has to do with those with a low IQ must have been busy, passed from the time of the *New World*'s record run to the next steamboat explosion. Then, on March 22, 1853, the *R. K. Page—ex-Jack Hays* —was plodding along, more or less minding her own business, when she fell in with the *Governor Dana.* As the latter appeared to have a spot more speed, the gauntlet was thrown down, and the two steamboats went to work, their pilots and engineers egged on by the cheers of their respective passengers. The *Page*'s engineer, whom a passenger had bet the cigars that he couldn't pass the *Dana,* found his professional honor at stake and cast about for something to increase the steam; his eye fell upon a cask of oil, which in no time at all was sluiced into the roaring furnace. It built up the steam, all right—so much so, in fact, that there was a deafening roar, and one of her boilers shot forward like a huge and lethal rocket, carrying with it important parts of the superstructure—and three trusting passengers, who were never seen again.

Just twenty days later, off Las Pulgas Ranch, the *Jenny Lind* blew up, killing thirty-one of her one hundred twenty-five passengers, most of whom were trapped in the dining room. She, however, was not a river steamer in the legal sense of the word, being on the San Francisco–Alviso Creek run, toward San Jose. So perhaps these thirty-one don't count.

Just to prove that 1853 was a bad year, the San Joaquin River put in a novel bid for fame by staging a double-headed steamboat explosion on October 18, the two being unconnected except by the general classification of too much steam and too little caution. At around 3:30 in the morning, the *American Eagle,* coming down from Stockton to San Francisco, blew up near Three Sloughs, killing five passengers[1] and wounding several others. At five o'clock the same afternoon the *Stockton,* bound up river from San Francisco, exploded, killing one outright, fatally injuring another, and badly scalding eight more.

With 1853 out of the way, the *Ranger* waited a decent eight days before making her bid for fame with an explosion which killed three and maimed five. She was a high-pressure boat—a fact which her low-pressure rivals took no great pains to conceal from the traveling public—and the coroner was of the opinion that someone must have turned cold water into her overheated boiler, which will do it every time. That was January 8, 1854—and January 19 was the day which is remembered chiefly for the blowing up of the *Helen Hensley*. Apparently they were going to get away from their San Francisco wharf, Benicia-bound, with something of a rush, and had built up a goodly head of steam in anticipation. At any rate, both ends of one of her boilers blew out simultaneously. Oddly enough, only two were killed. One passenger had the novel experience of being caught by a flying mattress on which he rode, à la Magic Carpet, through the air to the near-by wharf, landing a bit unhappy but not really hurt.

Winter passed into spring, and on April 15 of the same year we find the *Secretary* (which incidentally had inherited the engines from the wrecked *Sagamore*) gleefully racing some rival, each hell-bent on getting first to Sacramento. Between The Brothers and The Sisters in northern San Francisco Bay, the *Secretary* blew up, killing sixteen of her people and scalding thirty-one so badly that others died within a few days. At the inquest it came out that the engineer, a playful soul, had secured an oar and at the moment the boilers could stand no more was actually using it to hold down the safety valve. No doubt the surviving relatives were a bit perturbed

---

[1] Her boilers, they decided, had been made of "faulty iron"—a convenient way of laying the blame on someone too far away in the East to prove troublesome.

by this bit of engine-room buffoonery, but it is not recorded that anything was done about it.

The organization of the California Steam Navigation Company apparently had a slightly sedative effect on racing, for the rest of 1854 passed without incident. But the little independents still yapped at the heels of the wicked monopoly, and so racing and lax maintenance continued. January 27, 1855, in fact, saw one of the worst of the river disasters. At one o'clock in the afternoon, the *Pearl,* after a brush with the *Enterprise*—an independent from Marysville—was just nosing into her landing below the mouth of the American River, and most of her hundred or more passengers were crowded forward, each anxious to be the first to land. There was a rumble and a roar; a boiler, kicking loose from its foundations, ripped through the crowd, filling the air with steam, splinters, and mangled humanity, and plunged into the river some distance away. Fifty-six were killed,[2] drowned, or fatally scalded. Arising in its wrath, the *Daily Alta California* let down its editorial hair on the subject of steamboat racing in general and the *Enterprise-Pearl* affair in particular. In those robust days, the mere fact that a newspaper might lose a two-inch ad by expressing an opinion was no deterrent. The owners of the erring boats were advertisers; but the good old *Alta* poured it on, just the same. It must have done some good, for almost ten months passed before the *Georgiana* blew up, with loss of life, on November 23. So much for 1855. The next year saw but one fatal explosion; on February 5, 1856, the *Belle,* bound from San Francisco for Marysville, blew up at a point about nine miles above Sacramento, her list of a score of dead being graced by the name of her master, Captain Charles W. Houston.

Explosions which occurred at landings, or as engines were slowed down, were not unusual, and contemporary coroners' juries probably were right when they found that someone had forgotten, in these circumstances, to "relieve the steam," which otherwise

[2] In keeping with the quiet good taste of the time, the burial of the victims was set off by a funeral procession which included Governor Bigler, a Grand Marshal, seven volunteer fire companies, those members of the State Senate and Assembly who were sober enough to sit up, and all the available stagecoaches of both the Wells Fargo and Adams Express outfits.

would have passed normally through the engine. This at once brings to mind the *Contra Costa* which in 1859 was doing her bit as a pioneer in the ferry service between San Francisco and the East Bay cities. On April 3 of that year, she left Pacific Street wharf at 9:05 in the evening, bound for Oakland. Eighteen minutes later, having slowed to cross a sand bar, she blew up, killing six and injuring eighteen out of her 300-odd passengers. What caused the greatest sorrow, apparently, was the fact that among the dead was the vessel's bartender. When the clouds of steam cleared away, the pilothouse was blown forward, the stack lay over the port paddle box, and the supports for the forward part of the hurricane deck were blown away, leaving the unsupported deck to hang down "like the limber brim of a worn-out hat," as the *Alta* put it the next day. The master and engineer were arrested and held for $2,500 bail. At the inquest, it developed that she was allowed 65 pounds pressure, and had been carrying only 42 a few minutes before. This was brought out by a passenger, whose testimony revealed an oddity of the times: the *Contra Costa* had her steam gauge up on the main deck, for the amusement of the passengers. The jurors decided that the engineer had failed to relieve steam pressure by lifting the safety valve, as he closed his throttle. Despite the fact that the *Contra Costa* had been somewhat disorganized by the affair[3] she was rebuilt, reboilered, and put in service again.

On the morning of August 25, 1861, a small ad in the *Alta* announced that the *J. A. McClelland,* an "independent" owned by Captain C. Mills, was resuming service to Red Bluff. At one o'clock the same afternoon, while she was bound for that city and had reached a point a mile below Knight's Landing, one of her boilers let go. So powerful was the blast that her pilothouse—complete with Pilot S. Baldwin—rose to some altitude and dropped back into the texas deck, near the smokestack, with the startled Baldwin still intact. Fifteen people died in the blast, and eight others were more or less badly hurt. As the vessel was only eight

---

[3] The starboard boiler had followed the fashion of the day for such cases by skyrocketing clear out of the boat and sinking with a great hiss, some distance away. Later it was raised from the Bay and became Exhibit A for "the people."

months old at the time, some cause other than age of material must
have been responsible for the blast. Her hull, which sank in fifteen
minutes, appears to have been susceptible of salvage, for it lived to
ply the river again, as the *Rainbow.*

Nearly two years elapsed before the next disaster. Then, on
April 27, 1863, the *Ada Hancock* and some fifty individuals, at
San Pedro, passed into scalding memory. On October 26, 1864,
the *Sophie McLean* blew up in Suisun Bay, killing three. Another
year of peace and quiet—and then, some thirteen months apart,
came the horrors of the *Washoe* and the *Yosemite.*

The *Yosemite,* of the big line, and the *Washoe,* Captain G. W.
Kidd's "opposition" steamer, were rivals; in fact, the *Yosemite* had
once sunk the *Washoe* under conditions which caused some comment at the time but could not be legally established as smacking of
skulduggery. At any rate, the *Washoe* left San Francisco for Sacramento at four o'clock on the afternoon of September 5, 1864, eight
minutes behind the *Yosemite.* A reporter from the *Alta,* scenting a
race, interviewed Captain Kidd, who assured him that nothing
was further from his thoughts. So she headed into the stream, with
the *Yosemite* some distance ahead, as were the *Antelope* and the
Paul Pry. At 9:30 that night, when the *Washoe* was five miles
above Rio Vista, one of her boilers exploded without warning;
almost at once fire broke out in three places and her hull began to
fill. There must have been an alert lookout on the distant *Antelope,* for her master, Captain Foster, sized up the situation and
headed back for the stricken *Washoe,* reaching her in somewhat
over an hour. The ship was a shambles; of her one hundred fifty-
three passengers, sixteen were dead, thirty-six were badly injured,
and another fifteen had suffered minor injuries and burns. Neither
Captain Kidd nor Pilots Baldwin and Easton was injured, and
the mate, who had been asleep in his room in the texas, was blown
out of his bunk, fell through a hole in the deck—and escaped with
nothing worse than a bad shaking-up. The *Antelope,* with the
wounded and dead aboard, headed for Sacramento, her bell tolling
to indicate tragedy. After hanging up momentarily on a mud bar,
she reached the foot of R Street at 4:30 in the morning. Realizing

that something serious had happened, the Sacramento firemen had started tolling their own bell, and the town was out en masse. They set up an improvised hospital in the Vernon House in J Street, doctors and volunteer nurses were called in, and everything was done which was possible for the suffering victims. For the others, one of the era's typically gaudy mass funerals followed.

But California Steam was itself not immune from disaster. Shortly after six o'clock on the evening of October 12, 1865, the big *Yosemite,* running-mate of the *Chrysopolis,* was leaving Rio Vista, bound down river. She had been delayed some five minutes or more while the important paper work of settling the quarterly account with the postmaster was attended to, and her safety valve, set for 24 pounds, was blowing off. She was allowed 35—so either the valve setting was wrong or there was something else amiss. Her huge wheels had made less than half a turn when there was a rumbling roar, mingled with the crash of splintering wood and the yells of horrified humanity. The starboard boiler had gone, and the air was filled with live steam and the wreckage of her entire forward superstructure. Stanchions were blown away from under a deck on which was piled nearly a ton of gold and silver from the mines, and the precious cargo dropped into the hold. Oddly enough, Captain Pool, Pilot Enos Fouratt, and Clerk Johnson were all unhurt. Typical of the racial prejudices of the time was the *Alta*'s account the following day; it listed the names of thirteen American dead, and then added—just to keep the record straight— "There were twenty-nine Chinamen killed by the explosion, all of whom were buried at Rio Vista."

The *Chrysopolis,* Sacramento-bound, picked up thirty wounded and five bodies, taking them on with her. Just as the *Antelope* had done a year before, she solemnly tolled her bell as she approached the landing; once more Sacramento's volunteer firemen passed the word of disaster, and the *Washoe* proceedings were repeated. The inquest, as reported by the *Sacramento Union,* brought out the fact that there were "four cocks of water" in the boiler just before the explosion—that apparently being before widespread use of glass water gauges. They added that the boiler was made of "rather inferior iron," and, as several thousand miles separated them from the most interested party, hinted that this was because the iron was "made in England, by the Thornecroft[4] Mill." In a burst of patriotic virtue, the *Union* added: "The law now requires U.S.-made iron." All of the resultant lawsuits were settled out of court, and apparently the only legal action was the arrest of two deck hands who were caught in the act of robbing the dead.

The little high-pressure side-wheeler *Julia,* on September 30, 1866, had the first of her two explosions. She was bound up the river that evening, but had gone only as far as Alcatraz Island, in San Francisco Bay, when the chief engineer informed the master that there was something wrong with one of the boilers, and they turned back. As they did so, the steam drum blew out, killing five and scalding or injuring eleven others so badly that in several cases their casualties proved fatal. But that was only a foretaste of her real disaster, which came nearly twenty years later. In between, for the sake of continuity, was the only other bad explosion to occur; the *Pilot* blew up a few miles below Petaluma, killing seven men but not badly damaging herself, and, after repairs, spent many more years on the Petaluma Creek run.

It was dark—and densely foggy—as the *Julia* came alongside the South Vallejo wharf, at approximately 6:15 on the morning of February 27, 1888. Then those ashore heard, but did not see, a terrific explosion; in a few minutes' time there was a fluttering orange glow in the fog, for the stricken *Julia* was in flames, and was sinking. Not only that, but the wharf itself was on fire, adding to the difficulties of rescue parties who tried to get at the terrified passengers and crew. The lifting fog revealed the shattered hulk of the steamer alongside the wharf, from which arose billows of black smoke and sheets of flame. The *Julia* was an oil-burner—the first one, in fact, other than a few experimental jobs—and her storage tanks on the wharf were alight. Local journalists were not slow in picking out the fact that, instead of burning coal or wood, as any honest steamboat would do, she was flying in the face of Providence and taking the bread out of honest stokers' mouths by

[4] How the fine old firm of Messrs. Thornycroft must have loved that!

using oil; with nasty innuendo, they called attention to "the huge vats of petroleum" in her hold. There were some seventy people on board that morning, and thirty of them died in the flaming wreck. Sailors came down from Mare Island Navy Yard to help, and the firemen from North Vallejo drove madly to the scene, only to find that, as there were no hydrants and the tide was out, they had to wait several hours before deep enough water came in to permit the dropping of suction lines into the Bay and making a real attack on the flames. By that time, 600 feet of the wharf had gone. A few days later, divers scotched the story of the oil being responsible for the catastrophe, at least, directly: they found the starboard boiler ruptured and the port one blown out of the hull by the force of the blast, but the oil tanks still were intact. A dangerous seed, however, had been planted in the public mind, and the oil installations which were then being tried out in the ferry *Oakland* and the car-transfer *Solano* were at once replaced by coal furnaces.

Early on the morning of November 27, 1898, the big *T. C. Walker* blew up, about fifteen miles below Stockton, and killed nine men. So great was the force of the blast that the entire forward superstructure of the big two-stacker was demolished. She was successfully repaired, however, and ran for many years more.

That was about the last of the bad accidents. The loss of the *San Rafael,* in collision with the ferry *Sausalito,* cost three lives and the total loss of the *San Rafael.* The *Seminole–H. J. Corcoran* collision in 1913 was spectacular but not fatal. The *San Rafael* affair is of some importance in a literary sense, for it was upon this disaster that Jack London based the opening action of his two-fisted novel, *The Sea Wolf,* produced periodically as a Hollywood thriller, with varying degrees of success, ever since.

She was a cute little thing, was the *San Rafael*—a dainty single-ender with slatted paddle boxes, walking-beam engine, and a circular pilothouse like a ticket booth or kiosk at some bathing beach. And she probably was the last of the California steamboats to have the old-fashioned, wooden hog-framing. At the time—which was November 30, 1901—she was running as a ferry between Sausalito and San Francisco. She left Lombard Street wharf, loaded

Two old-timers at the Sacramento landing in the early days; to the
left are the repair-ways and shipyard at Broderick.

Davis Street Landing, San Francisco, showing the river steamer *Capital;*
in the foreground is the ferry *Contra Costa.*

Stockton, California, about 1860, from a contemporary lithograph

In the *Helen Hensley* the Mississippi River style of architecture was followed.

with commuters, and twelve minutes late for her regular 6:15 P.M. trip. There was a typical tule⁵ fog on the Bay, and she felt her way along slowly, pausing now and then to listen for the sonorous blasts of other whistles. Off Alcatraz one sounded close aboard; there was a blob of light in the dense murk, and a frantic exchanging of whistles between her and the stranger, which proved to be the *Sausalito*. The other craft caught the *San Rafael* right in the dining room, filled with passengers. Both boats were backing furiously at the time, but the little *San Rafael* was mortally hurt. The captains had the great good sense to pass lines between the two vessels and lash them together, or the loss of life would have been high. Hysterical passengers clambered on the *Sausalito,* as the other craft settled. A *San Rafael* fireman proved himself a hero by diving into her neck-deep fireroom to bleed the boilers, thus averting an explosion. Others busied themselves with rescue— and with trying to tell the ships' officers what to do. A minister of the gospel distinguished himself by storming into the *Sausalito*'s engine room and demanding to know why the whistle wasn't blowing, with all that fog on the Bay; his welcome must have had some of the aspects of the bartender's rush, judging from his complaint in a newspaper interview the following day. In twenty minutes it was all over and the *San Rafael* was hidden by twenty fathoms of chilly water, never to be seen again.

Nearly a score of years passed. Then the liner *Matsonia*—the old *Matsonia*—anchored one day, off Alcatraz. When it was time to get in her anchor, it came up slowly, breaking water with a mass of twisted, shell-covered ironwork — and a little brass eagle — dangling from its flukes. It was the eagle which completed the identification. The *Matsonia* had brought up a piece of the *San Rafael*'s engine.

⁵ Easterners and news commentators to the contrary notwithstanding, this is *not* pronounced "tool"; it should rhyme with "Dooley."

CHAPTER V

THE SLIM PRINCESS

WHEN YOU THINK of the California clippers, the name which first flashes across your mind is *Flying Cloud*; speak of the British tea and wool ships, and it is *Cutty Sark*. And just as each of these symbolized the finest of its class, so did slim, dainty *Chrysopolis* catch the fancy of the rivermen that even today she is remembered with affection.

Chrysopolis—the Golden City. It is, in fact, as the *Golden City* that Bret Harte refers to her in his impressive description of the great flood of 1861–62. It was an appropriate name, an outstanding name, even in an era when a man would go out and hang himself from a lamppost before he'd send a ship to sea with some such modern appellation as *Cities Service Koolmotor, Santacruzcement* —or *Sinclair Superflame*. Maybe it brought her good luck, for her life certainly was a pleasant and useful one, and when the floating palaces had had their day her soul marched on for more than half a century in another staunch and well-remembered hull.

John North designed and built her, for the California Steam Navigation Company, and both he and Captain James Whitney saw to it that nothing which went into her construction was anything but the best. Each stick of wood which formed the slender hull was the pick of the forests—and each piece was painted before it was carefully spiked into place. They intended that *Chryssie* should last a long time, which indeed she did. Her hull was 245 feet long, with a beam of 40 and a depth of 10 feet; she drew 4½ feet of water, and her tonnage was 1,050.

Below decks—or more correctly, through all of them—she carried a single-cylindered, vertical-beam engine with a bore of 5 feet and a stroke of 11, which rated 1,357 horsepower. There were two boilers, located on the guards,[1] weighing 32 tons each, and their working pressure was 55 pounds. Her paddle wheels were 36 feet in diameter, with 8-foot buckets, and even turning over at well under twenty revolutions a minute they gave her a speed which enabled her, on December 31, 1861, to come down from Sacramento to San Francisco in five hours and nineteen minutes[2]—a record which still stands. Her cabins were the picture of Victorian elegance — elaborately turned moldings, plate-glass mirrors, marble-topped tables, red plush upholstery, and glistening brass lamps. She could carry a thousand passengers and 700 tons of cargo, and her fuel capacity was 25 tons. Leading artists of the time were engaged to set off her interior with murals of California scenes—and all this for $200,000.

She was nearly complete as she stood on the stocks at Steamboat Point, on the moonlit evening of June 2, 1860. It had not been intended to make any particularly gala affair of the launching, being at night—but the word had got around. Sloops and Whitehall boats moved slowly before the launching ways, and there were crowds ashore as the shipwrights' mauls swung against the shoring. She quivered, and slowly gathered way down toward the water. In a few minutes, her tall slender stacks framing the brilliant moon, she was water-borne at last; then she was towed away to Benicia

[1] There was a popular tradition that, if the boilers were on the guards instead of inside the hull, the vessel might "blow up and be damned, sir," without causing the slightest inconvenience to the passengers. It was a pretty theory.

[2] She came by way of Steamboat Slough, cutting the distance down to 120 miles; her speed therefore was 22.7 m.p.h.—or 19.8 knots—which rudely upsets the popular belief that paddle-wheel vessels are necessarily slow.

for the final touches. Soon afterward she was regularly in service on the winding river. Captain E. C. M. Chadwick, late of the *Wilson G. Hunt* and the *Sophie,* became her master.

And so began a long and useful career. Every second afternoon at four o'clock, she would back down from the landing at San Francisco, swing majestically in the stream as her slender bow moved to the north, and then lay down a broad trail of white foam as she headed for the distant river. On the intervening days, it would be either the *Antelope* or the *Yosemite* which would leave at the same time, each vessel laying over at Sacramento and coming down the next night. One day of each week they were idle, and it probably was this necessary rest and chance for a bit of puttering around with boilers and engines which enabled the *Chrysopolis* to keep her youth. From the start, she seems to have had loving care bestowed upon her, as was befitting a lady of her station.

Others could go in for racing if they wished, but not the *Chrysopolis.* If she wanted to, she could show up the whole lot of them, so why strain herself in trying? She was content to dwell in the esteem and respect of her friends without getting her name into the papers in an unpleasant way, and her life passed in complete innocence of explosions.

And yet there was one explosion, but it wasn't her fault. As always is the case when there is a war on, you will find hordes of domestic Horatios ready to hold the bridge, provided the bridge is no farther away than, let us say, down at Rio Vista. Wherefore, both after the Mexican War and in Civil War days, the state erupted with a veritable rash of more or less official militia companies, many of which persisted for years as marching and elbow-bending societies. There were the Sutter Rifles and the Coloma Grays, and there were the Knight's Ferry Dragoons. A large element of the California population being, even as now, of Hibernian stock, it is not surprising that there also were the McMahon Guards and the Emmett Guards, which boasted two companies—one in Sacramento, the other in San Francisco. They held clambakes and free-for-alls and encampments, the latter always attended by some local Pooh-Bah, preferably with a military background. Before he marched away to the Civil War, to achieve fame as Fightin' Joe, General Joe Hooker of Sonoma County was much in demand as "Inspector" at the encampments of the more socially prominent companies. The Blue Book rating of these swashbuckling militia outfits was in many cases determined by the social standing of the volunteer fire company of which they often were an adjunct.

The Emmett Guards of Sacramento decided that St. Patrick's Day of 1869 would be an appropriate time to engage in a bit of serious wassailing and marching with their comrades-in-arms, the Emmett Guards of San Francisco. It was the misfortune of the *Chrysopolis* to be the down boat that night. During the day, two worthies attached to the outfit asked their company commander if it would be all right if they brought a small cannon with them. He stated flatly that it would not, and the master of the steamer backed him up. However, they were down nearly to Steamboat Slough before it was discovered that the pair had, in some manner, smuggled not only the cannon but also a keg of powder aboard. There was no more peace that night. The next morning when the *Chrysopolis* was approaching the wharf in San Francisco the two mountebanks loaded up for what they planned as a grand finale. It was. When the smoke cleared away—the keg as well as the cannon having gone off—a lot of planking was loosened, several of the nice red plush seats were on fire, and sixteen of the Emmett Guards were injured. Unfortunately the two who were responsible were not killed. That was her only explosion. The rest of her life on the river was one of gracious service, of comfortable speed, of meals which will go down in history.

But time was marching on; the railroad had come, and there was no longer a pressing need for fast and palatial steamers on the rivers. They sold the *Chrysopolis* to the Central Pacific, who planned to rebuild her as a ferry, for the San Francisco–Oakland run. That was in 1875. Her last trip, as a single-ended hull and with those huge wheels, was down to West Oakland, where her upper works were removed, the boilers were taken off the guards, and she was hauled out to where carpenters could get at her hull. When it was all over the metamorphosed *Chrysopolis* had seen her hull lengthened to a shade over 261 feet, and the upper works had been built out to where she was 72 feet over the guards. The boilers were in the hull, now, alongside the same faithful engine, and her wheels had been cut down to 28 feet but widened so that she swung twenty-four buckets each 10 feet wide and 28 inches deep. Her tonnage had gone up to 1,670 gross—and she was now the ferryboat *Oakland.* At high tide on June 2, 1875, she was launched; but she stuck in the mud, and it was not until two days later that they got her off.

There are millions who remember her as the *Oakland,* of the Southern Pacific system—even though she was extensively altered in 1898, and again rebuilt in 1920. Only a small percentage of her passengers, however, knew her real background. Those who stood, in curiosity, before her open engine-room door and watched the sedate rise and fall of the huge, foot-like "wipers" of her valve gear did not realize that they were gazing at the same machinery which had carried gold seekers to the diggings so many years before. Yes, in those days things were built to last. And so the *Oakland* carried on her new life on San Francisco Bay. Early morning commuters scurried aboard to get good seats in her excellent, fast-working dining room, to kill two birds with one stone by eating while on their way to work. Others sprawled on her benches, catching up with the morning papers, or stood on her broad decks to see San Francisco's magic skyline spreading out to envelop them. "Big Game" nights found her jammed with laughing students, and on calm summer evenings, quiet couples sought the shadowed benches of her forward deck, spinning their own dreams as the moon turned the Bay to a sheet of dancing silver. Ah, simple souls! Little did they realize that in a few short years they were to give all this up for bigger and better transportation—to be jammed like unwilling sardines into jolting electric trains, where the seats go to those with the sharpest elbows and the worst manners. Sometimes, if they were lucky enough to have a view through a window as the train sped across the bridge, her one-time passengers could get a brief, nostalgic glimpse of the *Oakland* lying, deserted, at a wharf far below. She may not have been fast, in this speed-mad age, but at least you could travel on her without having someone firmly planted on your feet, and someone else breathing bourbon and garlic on the back of your neck.

Even before the bridges came, the *Oakland* was allowed to relax, as an extra boat. She nearly ended her days in 1930, in a collision with the liner *Pennsylvania*—which did her very little harm but so frightened many of her passengers that they hastily scrambled up Jacob's ladders to the greater safety of the liner's high deck.

And then came the gaunt, gray bridge. The Slim Princess was old now—old, and just a trifle tired. The day of the ferryboat was done. True, they would need a little such transportation for meeting the overland trains, and some for the ephemeral traffic of the Exposition, but that could go to newer boats. There is no percentage in holding on to an idle steamer, even one in which lives the soul of the *Chrysopolis*. And so she was sold to the wreckers, to be broken up.

They towed her to Oakland, and the junkies took over. Out came windows, up came benches and linoleum, off came plumbing. Her massive ironwork would bow to but one master—the acetylene torch. And so came the morning of January 27, 1940. This lumber would bring so much, that metal would fetch a tidy sum; it was all figured out, and the deal would show a nice profit. There was a ready market for scrap, especially in Japan. But the Slim Princess was not to go that way. A spark from an acetylene torch found its way down into her bilges, now fouled with the oil-drippings of years. A thin wisp of smoke came up, there was a subdued puff—and she was all on fire inside.

A scared workman rushed to the little red box on the nearest street corner. Distant sirens rose in pitch and volume as engine and truck companies sped toward the now all-too-apparent column of smoke. Long snake-like lines of hose plopped, flat and lifeless, into the street, to become hard and round as the pressure went on. Helmeted firemen, heads bowed against the mounting heat, bored into the flames with heavy streams of water. It had little effect. A second alarm went in, and a third, as the menace to wharves and shipping grew. Over on the San Francisco side of the Bay the big fireboat *David Scannell* let go her lines and headed at top speed for the scene, her crew laying out gear and testing the valves of her huge monitors as she crossed under the shadow of the bridge, Oakland-bound. By noon they had the fire out.

Old sailors say that, on the last day of the world, all the remaining ships will be drawn by white silk towlines into the setting sun, to join those which have gone on before. There you will find *Thermopylae* rubbing strakes with *Golden Hind,* while *Lightning,* arisen from the fire, snuggles under the shelter of the murdered *Olivebank*'s tall spars. But it isn't limited to windjammers; steamboats can go there too—good steamboats. So, at noon of January 27, 1940, *Cromdale* and *Mary Celeste* and *Pass of Melfort* moved over a bit, to make room for the Slim Princess. And from that distant Valhalla to which are gathered the souls of all good ships, *Chryssie*'s gay spirit laughed down at that junkie.

CHAPTER VI

UP RIVER TO THE SOUTH

Steamers, after passing Chipp's Island, swung hard right for New York Slough, from which they emerged into the slowly flowing San Joaquin, and headed away toward the southeast through the maze of islands and sloughs of the Delta country, with Stockton as their goal.

Today, Stockton is a deep-water port, some eighty-five miles above the sea. But in the days of the Gold Rush steamboats, it was farther than that by a good many miles. Government dredges were yet to come, cutting straight tangents across the meanders and deepening the water so that full-sized deepwater cargo steamers can now come to the front door of California's progressive inland seaport.

It was on November 15, 1849, that steam navigation came to the San Joaquin River, advertising its presence in the boisterous manner of the time. Captain Warren, with the *John A. Sutter,* was the first to make it. The *John A. Sutter* heralded her arrival with a thrashing of paddles and a series of blasts from her whistle, and the whole town came running. They made her fast to an oak tree, at what later became the foot of Center Street, and tossed a gangplank ashore. Always the perfect host, Captain Warren invited all and sundry to come aboard and partake of his modest cheer. As the doughty captain's idea of modest refreshments included champagne, it is not surprising that the guests waxed enthusiastic, and if there was a sober adult male in Stockton that night it was because he had been unable to get to the *John A. Sutter*. Her enterprise thus launched in the bubbling juice of the grape, the steamboat was accepted with open arms and began to fatten the captain's bank account as she shuttled back and forth between San Francisco and Stockton with passengers, goods, and mail. Within a few months' time, as a matter of fact, the *John A. Sutter* had cleared a tidy $300,000; then, early in 1850, she was withdrawn for the more lush traffic of the Sacramento. But he was not a man to forget his early friends, was Captain Warren; and Stockton, having tasted the luxury of dependable traffic to San Francisco, had to be provided for in a proper manner. So, with some of the *John A. Sutter* profits, Warren bobbed up with a side-wheeler called the *El Dorado*. A newcomer, the *William Robinson,* appeared on the scene at about this time, and it looked as if the *El Dorado* might have a bit of nasty competition. But the *William Robinson*'s people were inclined to see things the right way, and she joined forces with the Warren boat, to the end that prices were maintained at a profitable level.

It is a basic law of economics that as soon as you develop a good racket some rank outsider has to muscle in. In this case it was a Captain Farwell, who entered the picture in July 1850 with a packet called the *Mariposa*. As a one-man opposition he took on the *William Robinson* and the *El Dorado,* free-for-all and no holds barred. Forthwith, the rates went down to within sight of, if not actually past, the red-ink level.

And now let us pause to reflect upon the ingratitude of mankind —especially when pecuniary interests enter the picture. Less than a year had passed, but already the gay initial entry of the *John A. Sutter* into their fair city was forgotten by the burghers of Stockton. Warren's champagne had flowed in vain, so far as the year of 1850 was concerned, and the merchants entered into a plot with Captain Farwell to show the wicked *Robinson–El Dorado* combine a thing or two. In short, they would give Captain Farwell all of their business, and Captain Warren could offer his champagne to the catfish if he were so minded. In the cabin of the *Mariposa* it was all solemnly agreed; Captain Farwell was, effective as of this date, the fair-haired boy and would get all of their trade. Consequently, for the next few trips the crews of the *William Robinson* and the *El Dorado* had no one to talk to but themselves, while the cut-rate *Mariposa* was loaded to the guards.

It is idle to assume that a man who can clean up $300,000 with a little steamboat in a few months is a soft or easy opponent. Warren's outfit immediately advertised that they would beat the tariff of the *Mariposa,* however low it fell. And that is exactly what they did. Captain Farwell became a most unhappy man, as one by one he saw the sturdy Stocktonians who had pledged undying support to his steamboat slyly letting their cargo get back to the combine. After all, it is hard to fight two steamboats with one steamboat, and the public is likely to turn to the cheapest service regardless of any promises which it has made. The fare to San Francisco got down to a dime a head, and then the combine announced that, to show their good will to the people of Stockton, anyone who wanted to go to the budding metropolis had only to step aboard and make the run as a guest of the line. Captain Farwell was about ready to fold up, after this last bit of economic shenanigan; but the people had now become river-minded, and it took three steamboats to handle the trade. And so, one wild night, there was a conference and much smoking of vile cigars, under the soft glow of the lamps in a steamboat's cabin. Then and there was born a new era in San Joaquin transportation—Captain Farwell joined the combine, with a solemn agreement that the rates would forthwith be hiked to a level where they all could make up what they had lost. This meant $12 for a deck passage to San Francisco, or $18 if you wanted what they laughingly referred to as a bed; and cargo was $20 a ton. The torrid air of the San Joaquin Valley was rent by the anguished howls of the merchants of Stockton, who, forgetting their own shabby treatment of Captain Farwell, now complained long and bitterly how he had sold them down their own river. They were learning, the hard way, that the buxom lass with the blindfold and the frequently maladjusted scales occasionally wins.

Back in the money again, Captain Warren interested San Francisco capital and, in November of 1850, went East to buy the engines and fittings—including the best of glassware—for a fine new steamboat to be named the *Santa Clara*. Her commissioning at Stockton was the signal for an outburst of arm-waving revelry which put the *John A. Sutter*'s coming-out party in the shade. Her life, however, was a short one; within a few months after her bibulous christening she was destroyed by fire. Undismayed, the captain got the *Jenny Lind*—of gory memory—and startled the natives by putting on, as a regular thing, seven-hour service to San Francisco with the trim little side-wheeler. In December 1851 the *Erastus Corning* and the *San Joaquin* appeared upon the scene, and the old story of rate wars had to be repeated. Deck fare to San Francisco went down to $1.50, and soon afterward the free-trip routine was repeated. The newcomers must have seen the light at about this time, because before very long the tariff was back at its old level and all hands—except the people of Stockton—were happy.

By early April of 1852 there were no less than seven steamers daily from San Francisco to Stockton, each vessel returning the following day. As the town grew, the trade expanded; and for miles the hot summer air carried the booming notes of steam whistles across the myriad islands of the Delta region, as side-wheel and stern-wheel vessels ran out of the fairways and into the snake-like bends of the river and its tributaries. Through liners like the *John Bragdon*—250 feet long, with a 9-foot draft and 35-foot wheels—made it in one leg; the smaller boats built up a lucrative trade by stopping off at the ranches and farms along the river and doing their part in developing one of the richest agricultural sections in the nation—a trade which was to endure for many years after the quest for gold had passed.

The formation of the California Steam Navigation Company in

1854, which had produced such a stabilizing effect on the Sacramento River trade, was to do equally well by the San Joaquin. Their rate of $6 a ton for freight to Stockton was just a third of what had been in effect before; but it seems that there always are people who are hard to please. Raucous demagogues assured the citizens of Stockton that they were the victims of the financial wolves of San Francisco and Sacramento and that they should arise in their might and do something about it. Sixty-four of Stockton's businessmen called a meeting, which turned out a crowd of eight hundred, to discuss ways and means. A committee was formed and the machinery for incorporation of an independent steamboat line was set in motion. The coast was scoured for available tonnage, and finally the former Oregon packet *Willamette* was acquired. Shouting their own praises, the Stockton merchants set forth to drive the slithering octopus of California Steam from their fair river. But the big company was no novice at this game; they all had come up from the creeks and sloughs to their present affluence by the knock-down and drag-out method. The *Willamette* was a push-over; it took a relatively short time for the line to break the back of the civic concern with its lonely steamboat and put river trade back on its old basis.[1]

The great flood of 1861–62 will be noted for, among other things, establishing steam navigation on the Mokelumne, a tributary which empties into the San Joaquin some eighteen miles above its confluence with the Sacramento. As navigable rivers go, the Mokelumne is no great shakes, having a course which would give an eel a nervous breakdown. But, with the roads all covered by deep and fertile mud, it offered a practical means of communication with the hinterlands—specifically, with the settlement of Lockeford, in which a Dr. D. J. Locke—an earnest gentleman with a Santa Claus beard, and a burning faith in temperance—was deeply interested, being in fact its founder and Number One citizen. So, early in 1862, he went to San Francisco and chartered a

---

[1] A quaint trick of this period was to buy up an asthmatic steamboat, put her on the San Joaquin at cut-throat rates, work up a good nuisance value, and force the established line to buy you out.

steamboat called the *Fanny Ann,* a 110-footer. His instructions to her master, Captain John Haggerty, were direct and to the point: Get up the Mokelumne to Lockeford, if it takes you two weeks. But Locke, it seems, was not the only empire-builder on the Mokelumne. In fact, to reach his own bailiwick it was necessary for him to pass the settlement of Woodbridge—and Woodbridge had been carved out of the wilderness by a gentleman named J. H. Wood who was as hard-headed as Locke. One of Wood's pet theories was that, so far as the Mokelumne was concerned, navigation ended at Woodbridge. Anyone who wanted to go farther could unload there, and he—Wood—was the one to see about getting his goods any farther upstream.

There is no reason to suspect that there was any understanding between this fresh-water Napoleon and the master of the *Fanny Ann;* but the fact remains that, on reaching Woodbridge, the worthy Haggerty announced in his best elocutionary style that he would "go no further on these perilous waters." At all odds, they dumped on the Woodbridge landing the whole of what, for want of a better designation, we may manifest as Cargo ex–*Fanny Ann,* Voyage No. 1, East-bound. Controlling his blood pressure as best he might, Locke went back to San Francisco and agreed to buy the double-engined steamboat *Pert,* Captain Allen, on the condition that she would get to Lockeford. The *Fanny Ann* had given up the job at Woodbridge on February 21, 1862; it was on April 5 that the *Pert* majestically steamed into Lockeford, to the intense satisfaction of her new owner, who handed over a check for $4,000 —which was cheap enough—and started the organization of the Mokelumne River Steam Navigation Company. Captain Allen was succeeded by Captain A. P. Bradbury, and the line expanded, buying up the *O. K.* and the *Mary Ellen.* The latter appears to have been a bit big for the job, for she never got beyond Woodbridge, and well may we imagine Wood tittering to himself as she made fast at his landing; the *O. K.,* for all her flippant title of perfection, got to Lockeford now and then but not with any great regularity.

During the next three years Locke's outfit did an excellent job of clearing the Mokelumne of snags and bars, for a considerable distance above Georgiana Slough. They formed the Mokelumne River Improvement Company, and started collecting tolls of ten cents a ton on cargo moving up the river. But success was of short duration; already the rich mining lodes were petering out; and then came the faster, more certain transportation offered by the new railroads. The Mokelumne steamers, one by one, were withdrawn, and the maritime history of the tortuous waterway, so far as steam-driven commerce on its upper reaches is concerned, came to a close.

At this period, of course, the Civil War was at its height. And those who think that California was out of the Civil War are entitled to at least one more guess. True, the California regiments which went off to battle were merged with New York outfits, and hence lost their identity; but the state was full of violent partisans on both sides, and the great struggle had its repercussions along the West Coast. Captain C. M. Weber,[2] "the father of Stockton," was a staunch supporter of the Union cause. On an island adjacent to his home he had erected the tallest flagpole which money could buy, and from its truck floated, after every important Union victory, a huge American flag. This so annoyed his Copperhead neighbors that, on several occasions, the halyards were cut and the flag torn down. Finally the worthy captain could stand it no more; he got a large dog, which had sharp teeth and no sense of humor, and turned it loose on the island. For a while, the flag was unmolested. Then, one morning, the captain found the halyards cut again. The dog was dead—which is not to be wondered at, considering the fact that his carcass contained about half a pound of buckshot, fired at close range. The rage of Captain Weber arose to majestic heights; he talked of armed guards, and of shooting at sight anyone found fooling around on Banner Island, as it had been named in honor of its flagpole.

[2] A contemporary photograph of his mansion on the river shows, in the background, a lovely little bark-rigged vessel at anchor in the river. The bark, apparently of about 300 tons, has awnings spread fore and aft for protection against Stockton's blazing heat. And she has, of all things, stern ports and quarter-galleries. Her story would be an interesting one.

Public opinion swung to his side. Cutting down the national colors was a mere whimsical prank, which anyone might excuse. Shooting a dog, however, was something else again—something which was not easily to be forgiven. And those Copperheads had shot the captain's dog, they had—the varmints!

Over Banner Island, the flag waved unmolested from then on.

CHAPTER VII

THE STEAMERS LEAVE AT FOUR

ʙᴀᴄᴋ ɪɴ ᴛʜᴇ ᴅᴀʏs when the Bay came up pretty well to where Montgomery Street[1] now is, San Francisco's water front was a place to be avoided on a dark night. Not only were the local *paisanos* inclined to be a bit free and easy with other people's valuables— and lives—but anything approaching a thoroughfare which would be acceptable today was unheard of. Plank roads and plank walks over the waters of the Bay were then the height of modern improvement; for those parts of the roadway which boasted an actual earth foundation, deep wheel-ruts were the prevailing motif, and the question of mud or dust was regulated entirely by whether it was winter or summer. There were storage hulks lying on the mud, the tide rising and falling inside the ones which had been there long enough for marine borers to do their work. Some of the hulks were rather well gotten up as buildings, perhaps one of the most noteworthy being the hulk of the ship *Niantic*—later the Niantic Hotel—its site still occupied by the Niantic Block. Such was the Embarcadero of the period.

Before the formation of the California Steam Navigation Com-

[1] The foundation of the Montgomery Block—citadel of Bohemianism—is reputed to rest on tobacco hogsheads sunk at the water's edge and filled with masonry, which apparently was a sound idea. At any rate, in the 'quake of 1906 the "Monkey Block" never batted an eye.

pany put things on a more or less businesslike basis, lusty and un-trammeled steamboat competition produced a situation around the landings facing on this sorry highway which can be described only as bedlamatic. Someone conceived the idea that 4:00 P.M. was the proper time for a steamboat to leave, and the public seemed to agree. The result was that the adjacent waters of the Bay around that hour were literally crowded with river packets backing down from their landings, maneuvering, whistling angrily at each other for right-of-way, and finally straightening out toward the north for the races which were all too popular.

Schedules published in the *San Francisco Directory* for 1852–53 show, for each week, twenty-eight 4:00 P.M. sailings from Pacific Street, Broadway, and Long Wharf. On Mondays, Wednesdays, and Fridays the *John Bragdon,* the *Wilson G. Hunt,* the *Antelope,* and the *New World* left Pacific Street for Sacramento. Simultane-ously, over at Long Wharf, the *American Eagle* and the *Sophie*—the latter under command of Captain E. C. M. Chadwick, later of the *Chrysopolis,* and proudly bearing the designation "U.S. Mail" —were getting under way for Stockton. On Wednesday after-noons the uproar was increased by the *Camanche*'s departure for Marysville—she made her other trip on Saturday—and the Friday fleet was augmented by one of the *Urilda*'s semiweekly trips to the same town. Departures on Tuesdays, Thursdays, and Saturdays at 4:00 P.M. were the *Confidence* for Sacramento and the *H. T. Clay,* another mailboat, for Stockton.

The few who did not fall in with the 4:00 P.M. routine were the *Jack Hays,* which started her weekly trip to Colusa at one o'clock each Tuesday, and the *Jenny Lind* for San Jose via Alviso at nine o'clock each Tuesday, Thursday, and Saturday morning; de-parture of the *Jenny Lind* was simultaneous with that of the *Union,* for Union City. In addition, the *Willamette* was advertised as leaving for Sacramento "every other day" at an unspecified hour, the *Kate Kearny* was running to Stockton but her schedule was not posted, and the famous Sacramento liner *Senator* was listed as "re-pairing"—perhaps undergoing alterations after her first coastwise service on the San Francisco–San Diego run.

To the newcomer not greatly affected by the desire for gold the city must have appeared a bit uncouth. In fact, a clear but not altogether complimentary picture was set down in the personal diary of the Reverend Benjamin Akerly, one of California's early clergymen. Fortunately for our purposes, the good dominie was not only a keen observer but, being a meticulous person, one who recorded —by name and running-time—the various steamers in which he traveled now and then to Christianity's outposts in Sacramento, San Jose, and Petaluma. But that is getting a bit ahead of his description of San Francisco, where he arrived in the ship *Mercedes* on August 28, 1857, having made the trip from New York by the somewhat indirect route of Cape Horn, Manila, and Hong Kong. River steamboating had calmed down a bit by then, under the enlightening influence of California Steam and a few rivals; but the city and its people were still colorful in a dismal way, and the four o'clock routine was still in effect. With sublime disregard for the opinions of future Chambers of Commerce and other professional Californians, he thus described the city:

Friday 28 .... nine A.M.—We are upon the city of gold and poverty and beards and goatees. Our first impression of this world-renowned city is that it must be a most miserable place to live in. As seen from shipboard, it has a shiftless and woe-begone look; miserable one-story houses founded on sand, with sand above and sand below, apparently requiring only the wind to blow and the rains to descend when the entire rookery of baseless fabrics might be swept into the sea. .... This portion [the business district, which he found slightly more agreeable to the eye] of the city, like Venice, is a daughter of the ocean; the streets and houses rest upon piles. Several of the streets in this section are shamefully and dangerously out of repair. Many of the planks are broken, forming trap-holes through which you can look upon the sea beneath, and through which, also, one might most uncomfortably drop, of a dark night, and thus ingloriously end his earthly career.

Four P.M.—We are aboard the steamer *New World* bound for Sacramento. The passengers are many; the males, mostly, mustached very fiercely and bearded very patriarchically. One young man, with a goatee and talma,[2] who renders himself very conspicuous and is evidently vastly

[2] A flowing cape of the "Curse you, Jack Dalton!" type.

in love with himself, attracts our attention above all others; upon inquiry we learn that he is a clergyman. . . . . May God grant him common sense.

Seven P.M.—We have made a landing at Benicia. It is here that the great seaport was originally located; but the proprietors of the soil were greedy beyond measure, and drove the early settlers to the high, sandy and barren hills upon which San Francisco stands. . . . . Eight o'clock P.M. —We are entering the Sacramento River which is here, as I judge, half a mile wide. The wind from the ocean is cold and raw. Eleven o'clock P.M., retired to sleep.

August 29, six A.M.—At one o'clock this morning we landed at Sacramento, the capital and second city of California.

Subsequent entries in his diary show that he was far more favorably impressed with Sacramento than with San Francisco, on this, his first brief visit. A week or so later he returned to the "rookery of baseless fabrics" in the *Antelope,* whose schedule called for departure from Sacramento at two o'clock in the afternoon, for an eight-hour run to San Francisco. Thus it appears that in the summer of '57 the *Antelope* was the running mate of the *New World* rather than the *Senator,* which normally alternated with her.

In her time the *New World* was classed, and not without reason, as one of the "floating palaces" of the river. It was small wonder, for in those days the dull monotony of the plywood bulkhead and the overhead of obviously unseasoned pine was yet to come. Too, the early river passengers were spared from riding in vessels whose interiors were done up in the neo-*maison-de-joie* architecture which later was to afflict ocean liners. Today we might consider them, perhaps, a bit overdone in the use of ogee molding and of windows outlined in blue and ruby glass, because just a few years ago we were told that it was smart and fashionable to regard anything Victorian as ostentatious, *gauche,* or just plain lousy. As this is written, it is permissible to regard some of the items of the Victorian era as quaint, or even fairly easy on the eyes; it is in the latter class that, for the most part, the interior decoration of the early steamboat belongs. At least, the shipwright and the carpenter of that time had a sound working knowledge of the basic principles of classical design and didn't invent new atrociana as they went along. Moreover, the painters had not yet learned what could be done by pouring a bucket of orchid paint into a barrel of orange and then, adding insult to injury, dusting the resultant surface with powdered aluminum.

On deck, the packets of that time relied upon well-kept white paint to set off to its best advantage the neatly mitered panels and the pointed slatting of the paddle boxes. Lower-deck railings were generally of simple square uprights, with four or five wide, slat-like rails to keep the customers from rolling off into the river; on the upper deck the railings generally were hammock-netted. Inside, turned moldings, panels of hardwood or honest pine tongue-and-groove laid diagonally, red plush upholstery, and gleaming brass lamps were the thing; doors were likely to have etched or stained-glass upper panels or neat louvers. If you looked closely at the California scenes painted on the panels at focal points of interest, you were likely to find them done by some well-known California landscape painter.

A favorite of the period, on the river runs north and east from San Francisco, was the *Wilson G. Hunt,* built in New York as a Coney Island excursion steamer, in 1849. Her white-enameled cabin was—with commendable restraint—set off with just enough gold leaf to be neat but not gaudy, and the stained-glass windows in the monitor of her main cabin were things of beauty. She came to California, cleaned up $1,000,000 in a year's operation, and left behind her fond memories in the minds of rivermen and travelers. In 1858 she went to British Columbia, where she ran between Victoria and New Westminster; then she was sold to the Oregon Steam Navigation Company and operated on the Columbia. She was rebuilt in 1865, went back to Puget Sound three years later, and about 1877 returned to San Francisco, where she ran until she was broken up in 1890. She registered 450 tons, with the following dimensions: length 185.5 feet, breadth of hull 25.9 feet, depth of hull 6.8 feet; her single cylinder had a bore of 36 inches and a stroke of 108. She was one of the few if not the only California steamboat to be equipped with a steeple engine, rather than the conventional walking-beam or the more modern, inclined type.

The *McKim* was hailed as the last word in steamboats when she went up to Sacramento in the fall of 1849, but her reign as a favorite was brief. She belonged to the period in which the screw propeller was a bit on the experimental side, and by no stretch of the imagination could she have been called swift. The *New World* caught the public's fancy with her record run in 1851, and three years later gave her publicity added weight by going up the river from San Francisco in seven hours and five minutes, on July 4, 1854, thereby beating the swift *Antelope* by an even half-hour. For more than ten years she carried a broom, proudly lashed to her jackstaff; then, at the end of 1861, the *Chrysopolis,* needled by this powerful rival, stepped out and set the record which remains intact to this day.

The *New World,* incidentally, was no stranger to the law courts. But, although she had succeeded in running out on the Gladstones of New York, she was years later to find her operations somewhat impeded by the legal profession of California. It seems that, in 1865, the California Steam Navigation Company sold her to Captain Lyle, on his solemn promise—appropriately backed up by a bond—that she would not reappear in California waters for at least ten years. So she headed out through the Gate, swung north past Point Reyes, left behind a foaming white wake along the California and Oregon coasts, and passed into the Columbia. For a few years—substantially less than ten—she operated there and on Puget Sound; and then, one fine day, what should slip back into San Francisco Bay but the old packet herself: she had been bought again, this time by California Pacific Railroad. The rail-line people, it appears, saw no valid reason why they should carry out the agreement of a former owner, especially when it meant keeping a good steamboat out of circulation. But California Steam, as has been hinted before, was not an outfit with which to get gay. They could hire lawyers, too, and good ones. Forthwith the stout Manila lines which secured her to her wharf were not the only reasons for her immobility; she was held there by injunctions as well. Attorneys—hers and the steamboat company's—shook their manes and howled. They produced the *Civil Code,* the *Penal Code,* the Ten Commandments, and the *San Francisco Directory;*

the air rang with objections, demurrers, motions to dismiss, pleas
in bar of trial, and a great deal of indifferently pronounced Latin.
Time marched on, and they were getting nowhere. Finally, California Pacific Railroad sold out to Central Pacific, and Central
Pacific bought out California Steam; thus plaintiff and defendant
became, as it were, one and the same, and the *New World* was free
to go and come as she chose. No one but the attorneys had profited
from the deal, and as quickly as they could her owners lighted off
her fires and put her back to work.

While on the subject of California steamboats which went north
it would be well to give brief mention of the later days of the
Yosemite's career. After her explosion in 1865, she was extensively
altered; a splice of thirty-five feet was built into her hull, and steel
boilers replaced the iron ones which had so miserably failed her.
In 1876—as the star of speedy river boats was fast setting—she was
again reboilered and also got new engines, the whole job coming
to $66,000 and making her good for seventeen miles an hour—
almost the equal of the *Chrysopolis*. But with the railroads cutting the river trade to ribbons it was a poor time to go spending a
lot of money rebuilding steamboats; and so *Yosemite,* for all her
new machinery, was laid up at Oakland for four long years. At
about that time Commodore John Irving, founder of Oregon
Steam Navigation Company, came along, on the make for anything fast and reasonable in the way of a steamboat. He saw the
Yosemite leaning forlornly against the piling of her wharf, and
snatched her up for about a third of what her last re-fit had cost.
Under command of Captain Charles Thorn, and with a chief engineer by the Glencannonish name of Roderick MacIver in charge
below, she headed for Victoria, B.C. Her upper deck was glassed
in forward, and for many years thereafter she faithfully served
travelers between Victoria and New Westminster. She came to her
end in 1909 when she stranded in Puget Sound. No mere toy, the
Yosemite was 283.2 feet long, with a beam of 34.8, and a depth
of 13.6 feet. She was 80 feet wide over the guards, her 32-foot
wheels carried 10-foot buckets, and her 57-inch cylinder had a
stroke of 122 inches.

No discussion of the river favorites, of course, would be complete without at least a brief description of the *Senator,* of which Derby[3] has written so delightfully in "Phoenixiana," mentioned, thumbnailishly, in earlier pages. From the time she first reached Sacramento, on November 8, 1849, she was popular. Brigantine-rigged, with a black hull, she was a handsome craft, and a money-maker. Under the going rates of the time, she charged a $30 fare, plus $10 if you wanted a berth instead of standing up all night; freight ran from $40 to $50 a ton. As a result, she showed net profits of $60,000 a month for her first year's service. As late as 1869 she was rebuilt, especially for the coastwise trade; when they got through with her, her old hog-frames were gone, the added longitudinal stiffening having been gained by raising her decks two feet eight inches, double-planking her, and renewing some of her more fatigued timbers. She was now 226 feet long, 30 feet wide, and 13.5 feet deep, and had a capacity of 1,012 tons of cargo and ninety-three first-class passengers. Her outside staterooms were done in rosewood, and the decking in her main saloon was of alternate planks of walnut and ash. Her bridal suites—of which there were four—were "beautifully and tastefully ornamented," as the *San Francisco Bulletin* remarked on June 6 of that year, in reporting her departure for Santa Cruz, Monterey, and other points south.

One wonders what became of the rosewood panels, the walnut and ash decking, and the "beautiful and tasteful" bridal suites when, a few short years later, she became an Antipodean coal hulk.

[3] Lieutenant George H. Derby, U.S.A., whose writings appeared indiscriminately under the pseudonyms of Phoenix and of John P. Squibob, brought joy to an otherwise drab world. During his interludes from the dreary "your attention is invited to Sub-paragraph 7-*f* of Reference (*A*)" and "you will explain by endorsement hereon," he not only produced "Phoenixiana" and a few riotous bits for the *San Diego Herald* but also found time to write a waggish letter to the War Department. In it he suggested that the pompons on the soldiers' shakos be replaced by oranges; his theory was that if hunger and thirst assailed the soldier he could eat the orange—which was not true of the pompon. The War Department did not take kindly to the suggestion, and Lieutenant Derby never became a general.

Chapter VIII

TRICKS OF THE TRADE

When Captain Enos Fouratt reached San Francisco in the schooner *Spray,* on January 2, 1850,[1] he had ideas about making a fortune by simply picking up the gold which he had been advised was lying around in chunks along the river banks. But Fate, the economics of river transportation, and a roving rattlesnake with a nasty disposition willed differently.

No sooner had he left the *Spray* than he was solicited to take the schooner *Chesapeake* up to Sacramento. The best information he could get on how to reach the up-river city was that it was "about two or three hundred miles away, in that direction," with a forefinger helpfully pointed in what might be termed a general

[1] She was actually off San Francisco bar on December 28, 1849, but adverse winds and currents robbed the captain, by a mere two days, of the distinction of being, like his brother John who had preceded him, a 'Forty-Niner.

northeasterly azimuth. This was a bit vague; the captain, however, realized that Sacramento was closer to the source of free gold than was San Francisco, and accepted the job. Forthwith he set about seeking more explicit sailing directions, and before long he met a chap whom he "had schoonered with on the Hudson," as he later described it. The friend had just returned from up the river, and for one reason or another he desired no part of Sacramento in the future; he did, however, pick up a pencil and sheet of paper and draw, from memory, a map of the winding waterway. With only this penciled sketch to guide him, the captain got under way with the *Chesapeake* on the morning of January 6, making the trip in about three days, and receiving, to his amazement, $1,600 in gold for his trouble. About that time he learned the only other way to get gold was to dig for it—which in no way bore out the stories he had picked up in the East. He was therefore in a receptive mood when a man came along and offered him $2,000 to take a brig down to San Francisco. The next morning there was a fine north wind, and on the strength of this he delivered the little two-masted square-rigger in Bay waters in a little more than a day's time. Another schooner was ready to go up, and for another $1,600 he took her to Sacramento. He picked up a few similar jobs in the immediate future; then, one fine day, the *Chesapeake* was put up at auction and he bought her.

Characteristic of the era's scorn for small change was the captain's subsequent flyer in dimes. Just as the professional San Franciscan of today insists belligerently upon wearing out his pockets with the proceeds of a ten-dollar bill changed into silver half-dollars,[2] so the local *paisanos* of the 'fifties would have no truck with any coinage other than gold. Another river captain had bought, on speculation, $2,000 worth of dimes—and found himself stuck with them. One evening there was a quiet little poker game, and as Captain Fouratt was as skilled in his handling of the traditional fifty-two bits of pasteboard as he was in matters of seaman-

---

[2] As good a way as any to get yourself tossed out of a Bay city taproom is to lay half a pound of your change out on the mahogany and say to the bartender that you'd really prefer to have American money.

ship, he became the possessor of the dimes. The loser was as well off as the winner, apparently; for those dimes did their new owner no more good than they did the other riverman. In fact, they lay around the *Chesapeake* in open kegs, and the playful deck hands used to pelt one another with handfuls of them. It was not unusual for them to sweep ten or twelve dollars' worth of dimes over the side when cleaning up in the morning. Finally the *Chesapeake* was sent up to Trinidad, during the Gold Bluff excitement, and was lost, dimes and all. At about that time the easy money appears to have played out and Captain Fouratt decided to have a try at mining. His career, however, was brief, ending when he stepped on a rattlesnake. The reptile, apparently quite willing to make an issue of the incident, turned around and sank its fangs into the doughty mariner. They patched him up, but the experience had chilled his desire for mining. And so he became pilot of his first river steamer, the side-wheeler *West Point*. That was in 1852.

In those early days, incidentally, the pilot did more actual work than the master, and got more pay; this was the case until about 1865. The Old Man's duties were largely administrative and social; it was he who entertained important passengers, lent his august presence to the dining saloon and social hall, and in general upheld the pride and dignity of the steamboat and her owners. Later, as master, it was not unusual for Captain Fouratt to entertain, at select and friendly little poker sessions in his cabin, groups of the elite which included such passengers as Stanford, O'Brien, and others who left their names in California history.

As has been hinted before, feeling ran high when the steamboats raced—not that this was unusual, considering the large amounts of money which frequently were wagered on the outcome of individual contests. It even got to the point of deliberate rammings if a rival proved too dangerous; there was, for instance, the night when the *Goliah* lay in wait in Suisun Bay for the avowed purpose of ramming and sinking the famous *New World*. But that steamer was as much too fast in battle as she had been in racing, and after a brief exchange of pistol shots between their officers and passengers the two vessels drew apart, the *New World* safely in the lead.

The famous race of the *Confidence* and the *Queen City,* while not featured by gunfire, nearly ended in flames so far as the latter vessel was concerned. The *Confidence,* of California Steam, burned Philadelphia coal, imported at some expense; the *Queen City,* which belonged to the Marysville outfit, depended upon the cheaper and more plentiful local supply of wood. So stern a pace did the *Confidence* set, for all the screams of her engineer about the speed with which his coal was disappearing, that the *Queen City* had to force her own fires until flame and glowing cinders poured in sheets from her stacks, the firebrands falling over her decks in a blazing shower.[8] Little fires broke out here and there, and it was necessary to organize her passengers into two work parties—one to pass wood to the furnace, the other to form a bucket-brigade and put out the resulting blazes on topside. But despite her efforts, the *Queen City* lost the race to her rival.

Around 1860, Peter Donohue built the *Sacramento,* primarily as a rival of the speedy *Antelope;* but as a racer she was a bit disappointing. One day the *Antelope,* which had left Sacramento half an hour behind her, caught up with the *Sacramento* at the entrance to the narrow channel of Steamboat Slough. The *Antelope* tried to pass, but the *Sacramento* "caught her suction" and forced her, crab-fashion, on to a mudbank, where she hung up. Captain Fouratt, who had her on that voyage, managed to get her off in a few minutes and started in hot pursuit; his passengers were very unhappy over the affair and began overhauling their six-shooters; but the captain assured them that he had an even better idea. Shortly after the two steamers had made their stop at Rio Vista he succeeded in jamming the *Antelope*'s bow into the *Sacramento*'s starboard quarter. The other pilot rang up full astern, hoping to slide off and rake the *Antelope*'s side—and, if possible, carry away one of her wheels. But the *Antelope* was turning up for full ahead, and all that the *Sacramento* succeeded in doing was to swing her-

---

[8] Later, when the towing of wheat-laden barges became more common, it was the practice to fit spark-arresters to the smokestacks. The boatmen didn't particularly care about the fires which they started in near-by wheatfields, but starting a fire on one's own barge full of sacked grain was something else again.

self squarely across her rival's bow. In that position the *Antelope* pushed her sideways down the river for several miles before they decided to call it quits. The next day, in San Francisco, Captain Fouratt was arrested on a charge of malicious mischief—a legal adventure which, he reported later, caused him "some slight delay and expense" but nothing really serious.

Pilots of the "Independent Opposition" steamer *Nevada* apparently delighted in "winging" the little *Antelope* and sending her home with badly tattered railings and joiner-work; but when they tried it out on the *New World,* they caught a tartar.[4] In their most daring encounter the high-sided *Nevada,* after trying to force the *New World* ashore, found herself hung up on the other vessel's lower guardrails, the *Nevada*'s superior height proving for once a distinct liability. Gleefully the *New World* pushed her on to a mudbank, only the skill of the *Nevada*'s pilot keeping him from the ignominy of being hung up in the branches of a huge sycamore, especially picked out by the *New World* for the ceremony. In a later race, the *New World* having chased the *Nevada* into Steamboat Slough at full speed, the leading craft's pilot, apparently with too much on his mind at one time, failed to note the slight swirl which marked a snag. There was a roar of splintering timber and the *Nevada* began to fill. They got her on a bank near Cache Slough before she went down, and so no one was drowned; but the bank proved to be quicksand, and the big steamer became a total loss. Some people maintained that, as her pilot had formerly been employed by the wicked corporation which owned the *New World,* he had done the whole thing on purpose; but nothing ever came of it.

Residents of the bustling village of Benicia, it seems, took their river racing seriously, and their sympathies appear definitely to have been with the opposition steamers. One fine evening, as the *New World* rang off her engines and drifted up to the wharf, the local peasants refused to take her lines. Meanwhile the rival *Washoe* was making a beeline for the same wharf, across the bows

[4] For taking similar liberties with the schooner *Mary A. Evans* in Carquinez Straits, the *New World* lost a $5,600 lawsuit on December 4, 1861.

of the *New World*. The latter's pilot—again the redoubtable Fouratt—gave her one bell and a jingle, and she gathered way, the two rapidly converging on what the best maritime circles recognize as a thing to be avoided—namely, the "collision course." The bow of the *New World* cut into the side of the *Washoe* as if she had been a pile of lug boxes, and it took no small amount of skill to get her ashore before she sank—which is fortunate, for the water off Benicia is not exactly shallow. Caught in flying wreckage, one of the *Washoe*'s passengers was killed, and the Benicians therefore had a virtuous angle to the rage which boiled over as a result of this treatment of the city's favorite steamboat; resentment was so high, in fact, that it was necessary to send soldiers down from Benicia Arsenal to protect the *New World* and her people from mob violence. The Solano County grand jury promptly indicted Captain Fouratt on a charge of assault with intent to commit murder, and he found it expedient to employ a mouthpiece—and a good one. The most important witness for the defense was to have been the *Washoe*'s pilot, and two well-known detectives of the period were detailed to see that nothing happened to him; however, one fine night he contrived to tumble out of his own pilot-house window and break his neck. In some manner not made crystal-clear[5] the case was disposed of, with no harm to the pilot of the *New World*.

The next year a new grand jury was called, and to the surprise of Captain Fouratt it indicted him all over again. The defendant and his legal talent did a bit of sleuthing and developed the fact that Solano County's face-saving gesture was not, strictly speaking, kosher. To be blunt, the whole affair was more or less a cooked-up deal, and one of the grand jurors was naïve enough to admit, under proper persuasion, that even before being called he had publicly announced that "the *New World*'s pilot oughter be hung!" With

---

[5] A quaint legend has been handed down to the captain's grandson, about this affair. It seems that the defendant assured the owners of his vessel that if he were advanced a modest sum in the neighborhood of $600 he could work wonders with the grand jury. Among the wonders he worked, it is alleged, was the roaring state of intoxication which he was able to induce in (*a*) the individual members of the grand jury and (*b*) the magistrate before whom he was supposed to appear.

such obvious malice on the part of at least one of the good men and true, the case was tossed out, and the incident was considered closed. The *Washoe* was raised and rebuilt, later to become Page One news by blowing up.

It was not until along in the 'sixties that anything serious was done in the way of charting the rivers. J. A. Crocker, carpenter for the California Steam Navigation Company, sounded the Sacramento early in 1863; penciled maps and personal knowledge on the part of the pilots had been all that there was for conducting a vessel safely along the Sacramento or the San Joaquin. If you wanted to get a vessel up or down, you were careful to entrust her to a man who knew just when to line up his jackstaff with this barn or that cottonwood in order to keep in the channel. The first printed chart came from data obtained, at about the time of the Civil War, by the brig *Lawrence* of the United States Revenue Cutter Service. The first charts listed the various important trees and houses and barns—and even, if we are to believe river lore, those homely detached structures immortalized by the late Mr. Chick Sale, if they were so located as to be of value as leading marks.

An early government-sponsored improvement on the rivers was a dolphin installed at the north entrance to Steamboat Slough, especially for the benefit of the huge *Capital*. She was so long, and so deep, that she couldn't make the short bend, and so had to go several miles out of her way, around the main course of the river. When the dolphin was in place she would ease up to it and, with her bow once set firmly against the piles, put the rudder hard over and come ahead on the engines. The result, of course, was that she would neatly pivot around on her bow until she was fairly on the new course; then she would back down just enough to clear the dolphin, give the "ahead" bell, and go merrily on about her business.

The value of the echo of one's whistle, in navigating close waters, is known to all pilots. But the Sacramento and the San Joaquin run through flat country, and to produce the required effect echo-boards were set up along the banks of the rivers. By giving a short toot on the whistle, and then listening for the echo, the pilot even in the thickest tule[6] fog could get from the echo-board a very fair idea not only of his bearing but also of his distance from it. The modern echo-boards generally are erected in connection with navigation lights, and are placed at strategic bends in the rivers, to assist the fog-cursed pilot in his work.

It is in the Delta country, and along certain reaches of the Sacramento, that the tule fog reaches its highest stage of perfection. Since the beginning of time it has had nothing to do but devote itself to the task of becoming a good, rousing, thoroughgoing fog—and it certainly has learned to do a workmanlike job. Yet in spite of these fogs and of the driving rain-squalls of the winter months, accidents have been surprisingly few. River seamanship is an art in itself, and any of the salt-water brethren who are inclined to look down their noses at river pilots are invited to try it themselves sometime, preferably with a vessel of no great value. The river pilot must know all of the answers, and know them right now.

Some mention has been made of the need for a certain knowledge of legal procedure—as, for instance, in the case of Captain Fouratt's difficulties with the grand jury. Captain Wakeman, of the *New World,* was a good side-wheel barrister, too—he had to be. The question has been raised from time to time as to how he managed, after snitching the *New World* out from under the nose of the sheriff on the East coast, to get her into other ports, including San Francisco, with no papers. Apparently the same thought troubled Captain Wakeman. So, it seems, when they got to Montevideo he signaled a boat, and started for shore, to call on the American consul. As soon as the boat was clear, he calmly arose and stepped over the side; the oarsmen, a bit puzzled, hauled him aboard and continued on to the landing. A few minutes later, dripping wet, he stood before the consul; he had met with a most unfortunate accident—in some manner he had fallen out of the boat,

---

[6] A Grade-A tule fog is so thick and so wet that it actually will put rural telephone lines out of commission, by grounding out the wires carried on merely rain-proof insulators.

The *Dover*, towing a barge by a line from her hog-post

Navigation on the San Joaquin, near Fresno, about 1905

and in doing so had lost all of the ship's papers. Would the consul be able to fix him up with a new set? The consul took it, hook, line, and sinker, and the worthy captain went back to his ship with all of the papers he needed.

The introduction of barges into the river trade presented a problem in seamanship which the rivermen were not long in overcoming. With a stern-wheeler, of course, you have no place to put towing-bitts. And even if you did secure them to the big beam abaft the wheel, you then would have them so far aft that your towing vessel would be unmanageable. Any towboat man will tell you what is meant by "getting in irons" with a tow—briefly, having the strain so far aft that the rudder is powerless to swing the stern against the weight. The British recognize this fully, which is why British tugs have the towing-bitts practically amidships. The better American tugs, both commercial and government, also have the bitts or towing-engine as far ahead of the rudder as practicable. But you can't do it in a stern-wheeler—the wheel is in the way; and that is that. Those barges, however, were there to be towed. What to do? Some imaginative riverman looked aloft and found the answer—the main hog-post. And so to the system of hog-framing which enables a river steamer to keep her lines and not sag at the bow or stern was added the job of taking the tow.

Steamers which might expect to do towing jobs were therefore fitted with a special bit of blacksmithing atop the center hog-post. It was swiveled to swing from side to side, and from it hung a wire pennant with a heavy wooden toggle spliced into its outer end. There was an eye-splice in the barge's towline, through which the toggle was slipped. Thus hooked up, steamer and tow would get under way; when they wanted to let go, the steamer slowed down until the barge slackened up her line, the toggle was then slipped out, and the barge drifted in to its landing. Incidentally, the *San Joaquin No. 4,* touted at the time of her building as "the most powerful inland vessel in America," towed as many as five barges, tandem, at one time.

The towline from overhead, incidentally, served another highly useful purpose. Obviously, with a galley and a cook aboard the steamer, it would be wasteful to set up similar arrangements in each barge, and yet barge crews get just as hungry as those aboard steamers. Hauling in the barges would be difficult, and thus another river gadget came into use—the towline dumb-waiter, operated like a breeches buoy, for passing food to the men who handled the huge steering-wheel and triple rudder of the barge.

As each meal was prepared aboard the steamer, it was placed, a dishful at a time, in a deep iron bucket. Then the bucket was secured to a snatch block on the towline, and the cook, standing on the texas deck just over the wheel, would solemnly pay out on a hand line fastened to the bucket. As a result, the barge crew's meal would safely pass aft along the towline, to be taken aboard by its ultimate consumers; and, after the meal, the same hand line would haul back the bucket and its load of empty dishes.

While on the subject of stern-wheel logistics, it is well to mention briefly a legend concerning the *Gold*—the original *Gold*, built in 1883 and not "The New *Gold*," which entered this vale of tears in 1889 as the scow *Fort Bragg* (named for the little coastal lumber town where she was built). The *Gold*, it is alleged, had a stern wheel which was innocent of any guard over its top. As a result—so the story goes—in among the myriad islands and sloughs of the Delta country she used to shuck catfish up on her texas deck, where they were picked up by the cook, skinned, and prepared as only that particular cook could prepare catfish. It should be made clear, however, that this story is not documented; it is merely a riverman's yarn which you are at liberty to accept or discard.

Chapter IX

THE RIVER HAS TEETH

$\mathcal{S}$AID THE PILOT, pointing off to port as the *San Joaquin* passed Walnut Grove, "That's Georgiana Slough." He gave the steering gear a touch, the wheel spun, and the bow moved slightly in the opposite direction. "You can go down to Stockton that way. It cuts over into the Mokelumne and comes out into the San Joaquin down around Bouldin Island. It isn't too good an idea, though; too many snags."

But Georgiana Slough isn't the only place where snags have arisen to curse California's rivermen. Both the Sacramento and the San Joaquin—to say nothing of the others—are fairly well lined with cottonwoods and sycamores and willows. They're beautiful things while standing, and anything but beautiful if they tumble into the river. The stream changes its course, or the water rises suddenly, perhaps just when a "norther" is blowing—and a tree topples over into the water. As it rots and becomes water-logged, of course, it disappears from view, and is not discovered until some luckless craft runs onto it.

Add to the snags the trees and brush hanging over the water in many places, and you will see one reason why, as the river narrowed or shoaled, side-wheelers yielded to vessels with a single wheel aft, more or less out of harm's way. Unregulated hydraulic mining filled the river courses with debris—this was the most important reason for discarding the side-wheelers — and forced adoption of the flat, box-like hulls in which every foot below the waterline is working uniformly for buoyancy.[1] Except away up forward, and for a short run before you come to the multiple rudders, there isn't much shape to a stern-wheeler's hull. In spite of this skimming-dish contour, however, many a stern-wheeler experienced the ordeal by snag, frequently with fatal results.

The dubious honor of being the first California steamboat to be snagged probably goes to the *Edward Everett Junior,* a quaint little thing which came out, sectionally, in the ship *Edward Everett* in 1849; in fact, much of her carpentry was done aboard the windjammer for which she was named and which was, in fact, a sort of floating shipyard. The little 50-footer was, incidentally, a stern-wheeler, and probably could have been floated on a few buckets of water. In spite of this, however, she got it—a snag through the bottom—in the American River, where the *Lady Washington,* San Francisco-bound from Coloma, also was snagged on her first voyage. A third vessel to be snagged—permanently—in 1849 was the side-wheeler *Pioneer.* The little *Plumas,* a stern-wheeler of only 51 tons, went out by the snag route in 1854, in the Sacramento.

The end of the *Nevada* came, as has been mentioned before, when she struck a snag while racing; for years, there were a few traces of her bones near the point where Cache Slough and Steamboat Slough empty into the Sacramento, not far from the town of Rio Vista.

On the night of October 18, 1870, the little steamboat *Belle* was bound down-river from Hovell's Landing and had just come out of Horseshoe Bend when she encountered one of the early hay schooners. Softly cursing the law which gives a sailing vessel the right of way, the *Belle*'s skipper rang off his engines and maneu-

---

[1] The 150-foot *Red Bluff,* built at Sacramento in 1894 for the up-river service, had a hull which was only 3.2 feet deep, and her draft was a thing which one discussed in inches if at all. She could—so they said—run wherever the ground was a bit damp.

vered to give the schooner room. As he did so, the *Belle* found a snag, which poked a hole through her side. Although the shock was not great, the wind[2] took a hand in the proceedings, and heeled her over to the side where, just at the waterline, the snag had gone through. There was a cheerful gurgling sound, and the *Belle* sank in 15 feet of water. Although she was only five years old at the time—which isn't much for a steamboat—the job of salvage must have been too much; at any rate, we hear no more of the *Belle,* and in the next listing of merchant vessels you won't find her. This is not, however, the reason why the name *Belle* has been immortalized in stone. The monument on the levee, at what since has become known as Monument Ranch, a few miles north of Sacramento, commemorates an earlier *Belle* disaster, having been erected in memory of one Leonidas Taylor, a young passenger killed in an explosion aboard the *Belle* several years before her demise.

As a result of numerous snag incidents, the federal government has maintained snag boats on the rivers for many years, perhaps the most famous being the old stern-wheeler *Seizer,* of Victorian—and later—memory. She was dismantled in 1921, to be followed by the square-bowed *Bear,* built in 1921 and dismantled five years later, and by the *Yuba,* built in 1925 and tied up, more or less "in ordinary," at Rio Vista in 1943.

Captain "Rush" Fisher, a gigantic Missourian, was the *Seizer's* master for a long time; and many are the tales which are told of his skill both in seamanship — or rivermanship — and in yarn-spinning. His crew always included a number of Kanaka divers, who, without the aid of any modern diving equipment, would plunge from the deck of the *Seizer* into the swirling, muddy current, to attach chains to sunken snags. Apparently, the copper-skinned divers were a bit "prima donna-ish," a condition which grew as they ended their winter hibernation while the boat was laid up and got back into the routine of eating regularly.

"Those Kanakas," observed Captain Fisher, "just lie around Sacramento and starve all winter. But as soon as they get the

[2] From below Collinsville to above Rio Vista, the wind, night or day, for about nine months out of the year, is enough to blow your hair off.

wrinkles out of their bellies—why, they act like the sugar on the dinner table was salt!"

It fell to the lot of the *Seizer,* on one occasion, to get squarely into the middle of a steamboat-railroad controversy; that was away back in 1892, when the vessel was commanded by Captain Demerritt. It seems that in an attempt to open river trade to points in northern California and southern Oregon, Captain J. H. Roberts headed up-river in the *Jacinto.* By this time, of course, the railroad had been built through to many of the northern points, and there was a drawbridge across the river at Tehama. The railroad people saw no reason why steamboats should be allowed to cut in on their business; as a result, when the *Jacinto* reached Tehama and whistled for the bridge to open, nothing happened. It then developed that someone had carefully spiked railroad rails across the joint in the draw so that the bridge could not be raised. Getting no satisfaction from the railroad people, Captain Roberts took his troubles to the *Seizer,* which chanced to be near by. Captain Demerritt listened patiently, put on his hat, and went over for a little chat with the local officials of the line. He explained to them that he was a kindly and reasonable man; he would, therefore, wait for all of three hours before he dynamited their bridge for them. Of course, if during those three hours the new rails were removed and the span were opened, it was entirely possible that he wouldn't have to use dynamite at all . . . .

In comfortably less than three hours, the span, hastily freed of the rails and spikes, opened up, and the *Jacinto* triumphantly steamed past.

One wild night in 1908 the *Seizer* left Sacramento bound up-river, with a barge and a snag scow in tow; the latter, representing someone's idea of how to save money, consisted of hull, boiler, derrick, and everything else except motive power—it was necessary to tow it to the point where it was to be used. For its crew and the Army engineer in charge there was a fairly comfortable cabin built on the upper deck.

As the procession bored on into the night, a "norther" grew in force. Finally, boat and tow entered a twist of the river known as

Wild Irishman Bend, in the general vicinity of Knight's Landing. And just after the towing vessel passed a big sycamore, the tree toppled over. The first thing that those aboard the snag scow knew they were pulled in under the branches; there was a splintering crash, and the whole upper structure, containing eight men, plunged into the river. They all got out through the skylight and swam ashore on the west bank of the river.

The spot where they landed, over by the Sutter By-Pass, was, at that time, unreclaimed. It was, in addition, fairly well grown over with wild rose bushes. Up to this point, the eight castaways regarded the whole affair as something of a lark; but it is remarkable how quickly one's sense of humor fades, as a result of standing, barefooted and in a wet nightshirt, in the middle of a patch of wild roses—with a Sacramento Valley "norther" blowing. In growing dismay they saw the steamer's lights pulling away, up the river; then came a ray of hope, for she gave a toot on her whistle, and there were signs of activity aboard. It developed that the cook on the scow, who was sleeping on the lower deck and so merely had the roof torn away from over his head, had finally, by his shouts and the waving of a lantern, aroused someone on the barge ahead, who had in turn passed the word on to the steamer. Before long, the eight barefooted castaways were rescued from their bed of roses and returned to the less romantic but definitely more comfortable cabin of the steamer.

It was in Georgiana Slough that the loss by snagging of the last large steamboat occurred—the *Neponset No. 2*, on November 2, 1921. Poking around, in and out among the various farm landings there, the old stern-wheeler took one right through her stout planking, and quickly settled to the bottom. What with the cost of salvage, the even-then waning glory of steamboats—and the age of the *Neponset No. 2*—they decided to leave her alone.

And so the government snag boat, whose efforts to make things safe for the steamers had been unavailing in this case, was called in to perform the last rites of clearing an obstruction to navigation. She pulled the *Neponset No. 2* apart and tossed her up onto the bank, where she no doubt provided some very excellent firewood.

Chapter X

UP BAR! DOWN BAR!

$\mathcal{W}$HATEVER may have been the faults of the old walking-beam engines of the early river boats, one never could use the overworked expression "streamline" in referring to them.

The Southern Pacific ferries, the *Sacramento*—which started in business as the *Newark*—and the *Eureka,* nee *Ukiah,* carry down to Californians the last example of this Rube Goldbergish bit of marine engineering. Passengers bound to and from the trains at Oakland pier[1] pause before the big plate-glass window on the upper deck, or at the open door to the warm, oil-pungent engine room, to

---

[1] This is the only ferry traffic permitted on San Francisco Bay. When the bridges were built, investors in the enterprise were given life-long protection by a conveniently passed state law which forbids any vulgar boatman from competing with the bridge-borne traffic. Certain cynical strap-hanging commuters have since expressed the view that such a deal may not have been the acme of wisdom.

gaze in brief curiosity at the slowly moving masses of steel which transfer the power of the single cylinder to the massive crank and the paddle wheels. They are looking at a type of engine a century old. Why is such machinery still found today? Well, in the first place, it is remarkably efficient; in the second place, turning only nineteen revolutions a minute and using a steam-pressure of only fifty-six pounds to the inch, it does not wear out rapidly.

The walking-beam engine consists of cylinder, valve-gear, beam, and crank. That is about all. The walking beam is slung in trunnions at the top of the massive, A-shaped gallows frame which projects above the weather deck of the cabin, and serves a dual purpose; it actuates the wheel crank and also operates the air pump. An eccentric at each side of the crank connects with a rocker shaft in front of the cylinder, by means of steel hooks which are dropped to engage two cranks. Four comma-shaped steel "wipers" are fixed to the rocker shafts, and as they swing up and down they lift the "toes" on the valve rods, and so operate the four poppet valves— top intake, top exhaust, bottom intake, bottom exhaust—when the wheel is turning fast enough to do the job.

Starting, stopping, and reversing require engine-room calisthenics which must be seen to be appreciated, for at these times the engine is valved by hand. Then the hooks are raised from their cranks and the rocker shaft hangs free. The engineer, by means of a steel bar as long as himself, turns a shaft at floor-plate level which opens simultaneously an intake valve and the opposite exhaust valve. There is a subdued roar of steam, and the big piston moves. He watches carefully, and when he sees that it has reached the end of its stroke—the idling hooks are his best clue to this—he throws the bar in the opposite position and thus reverses the pressure from one side of the piston to the other. Up bar! Far overhead one end of the walking beam rises to its limit. Down bar! And back it comes. In starting, this goes on until the momentum of the wheels is sufficient—to half-speed or better. Then the hooks are dropped onto the cranks—a movement which must be nicely timed—and the eccentrics relieve the engineer of his work.

When the hooks are down and the vessel is proceeding normally, the intake of steam at each side of the piston is cut off at about one-third of the stroke, leaving the steam to exert its full power in expanding, and thus utilize every ounce of its effective energy. It's the same idea as the big liner's triple-expansion engine, only that it is done with one cylinder instead of with three. When valving by hand, the steam is admitted for the entire length of the stroke. The reason for this is simple: In overcoming the inertia of the huge wheel, or in turning it against the forward motion of the boat in landing, it takes full pressure on the entire stroke to keep things moving. When finally under way, with momentum to help, you can drop the hooks[2] and take advantage of the steam's expansive power. Incidentally, they were not rigged uniformly; on some boats, it was up bar, up crosshead; on others it was up bar, down crosshead. An engineer on a relief shift was a most unhappy man.

On most walking-beam engines, while the engineer is doing his "daily dozen" with the "Johnson bar," his assistant—or he himself if they are short-handed—is busy with the burnished-steel wheel of the condenser valve. Most of these engines carry jet condensers—that is, the exhaust steam enters a chamber into which jets of cold water are turned to condense the steam itself into water; then the whole thing is pumped overboard. When the main engine is turned off, the condenser likewise must be shut down, to keep it from flooding.

The earliest steamboats were of the noncondensing type—that is, they exhausted into the atmosphere and the term "puffing like a steamboat" was no idle simile; they shot their jets of exhaust steam into the air as they paddled along. Surface condensers—where the steam is condensed by passing around a myriad of brass tubes full of cold water—were first used in the *Apache,* the *Modoc,* and the *J. D. Peters.* In this type of condenser, the condensate flows on into the hot well, from which it is pumped back into the boilers by a feed pump. In the old *Julia,* and several others, there was a system of exhaust pipes running around inside the paddle boxes,

---

[2] The expression "hook 'er up" to denote an increase in speed comes to us directly from the engine room of the side-wheelers.

where water splashed up by the wheels cooled them and thus served the same purpose as the cold water pumped through a normal surface condenser by the circulating pump. The *Apache* and other stern-wheelers each had a combination circulating pump and air pump, driven by the same single, auxiliary cylinder.

Hanging on dead-center is one of the perils of the walking-beam type of engine, which is obvious when you stop to consider the fact that you are dealing with one lone cylinder and hence have no chance for offset cranks; this is just another reason why the engineer has to be most meticulous in the handling of his valves. If the engine sticks on center, the only thing to do—if you haven't rammed through a pier and sunk yourself—is to break out the big, long, wooden bar which is kept for that purpose, get into the paddle box, and pry the wheel over. This is not as simple as it sounds—nor as safe. If, owing to a leaking valve, there is steam in the cylinder, the minute the crank crosses center it takes charge. Maybe it will go only a quarter of a turn, but that is plenty; if you don't get your bar out of the wheel in time, there is an excellent chance that both you and the bar will be hauled around inside the paddle box, and you'll be lucky to get off with broken legs.

The dead-center problem was present also in the steeple engine[8] and in the one with the single horizontal or inclined cylinder. With the more modern stern-wheelers, of course, there was no such trouble, for here there were two cylinders and two pistons; the cranks were offset, and as a result you could get positive action out of at least one of them, regardless of the position of the wheel. In some stern-wheelers, there were two separate, independent engines; more common was the cross-compound, in which the exhaust steam from the high-pressure cylinder on one side of the boat is piped into the low-pressure cylinder on the opposite

[8] The only recorded use of one of these odd engines was in the famous old *Wilson G. Hunt*. From outside, it looked as if they had built the gallows frame but had forgotten to put on the walking beam. Inside, the cylinder was to be found under the center of this frame; the piston worked vertically to a crosshead, sliding up and down in the frame, and from the crosshead hung two connecting rods which turned the port and starboard wheels as the piston went up and down—in reality, a form of side-lever engine.

side. The cranks are, of course, offset, and a by-pass permits admitting steam to the low-pressure cylinder should the high-pressure, or first cylinder, chance to be stopped on center. Both the *Julia* and the *Amador* had two independent, poppet-valve engines, although they were side-wheelers. The elaborate compound engines of the huge *Alameda* and the *Santa Clara,* resurrected for shipyard ferry service to relieve the wartime congestion of other travel, also carry independent engines, and can actually be steered by their wheels.

The later stern-wheelers of the California Transportation Company and of the California Navigation and Improvement Company used double-seated poppet valves of the "California cut-off" type; and in Southern Pacific stern-wheelers, after 1881, slide valves like those of a locomotive were used, except on their last steamers—the tandem-compound *Navajo, Seminole, Cherokee,* and *Fruto.*

With the passing of the side-wheeler, the reign of the low-pressure steamboat ended on California rivers, and boiler pressures ranging from 150 to 220 pounds came into practically universal use. It may seem strange, but this increase in pressure did not bring more accidents. For one thing, the low-pressure jobs belonged to the devil-may-care period of steamboat racing—and to the era of iron, rather than steel boilers. Safety kept well in advance of pressure. As a matter of fact, anyone who thinks that low pressure is innocuous is invited to take a jaunt out to Sutter's Fort, in Sacramento; there he may see a part of the torn shell of the *Washoe*'s boiler, which launched an impressive list of persons into scalding eternity. She was low-pressure, and not very far advanced from the days when they ran steamboats with pressures as small as 10 pounds.

Before passing to the related matter of river-boat fuel, it is interesting to explore briefly the possibility of a single-cylinder stern-wheeler—strictly, in modern times, the result of accident—and to recall what happened to the *Petaluma* one fine night a few years ago. She was plugging along across San Pablo Bay, bound for Petaluma Creek, when there was a resounding crack: the port crank of the paddle-wheel had crystallized and broken off. Fortunately for all concerned, the crank was at the bottom of its orbit, and so, instead of tearing out the whole after-end of the boat, the end of the crank, accompanied by the connecting-rod and certain important fitments of the high-pressure cylinder, merely sailed gaily out under the fan-tail and plunged into the Bay. They shut off the escaping steam—and at last the escaping profanity—and with only the starboard cylinder[4] in operation they worked her all the way up to Petaluma; the following day they got her back to San Francisco in the same manner. Divers recovered the broken crank and connecting-rod and patched her up. A few days later, you wouldn't have known that anything had happened.

Less fortunate was the *Modoc;* her piston rod carried away on the in-stroke, and the piston wound up among a lot of cargo in her freight deck. It was to guard against any such affairs—the *Herald* and the *Acme* also had drawn attention to themselves with broken cranks—that the modern *Delta King* and *Delta Queen* carry cranks cut out of huge steel plates, not forged.

In the early days, wood was the fuel of the steamboats. Cottonwood gave a fierce, hot fire—but one which had to be replenished continually. River oak was used to some extent; and so was bull pine, a favorite fuel, which, like cottonwood, was cut in four-foot lengths. But bull pine also was an excellent fuel for locomotives, and as the railroads pushed farther into the newly opened country most of the bull pine went up through the balloon-top stacks of the early engines. The boats operating above Sacramento used wood until about 1904, when everything was converted to oil.

How much wood did a steamboat take? Well, engineering data have not been entirely preserved; but a few notes have come down from the old *Dover,* which reveal that on a 48-hour run from San Francisco up to Butte City she consumed 48½ cords of wood; by the time she got to Colusa, 27 cords had gone up in smoke, so it must have taken her about 27 hours to reach that city, burning, let us say, a cord an hour.

---

[4] She had inherited this cylinder from *Petaluma* (No. 2)—ex-*Resolute*—when the latter burned in 1914.

Meanwhile there had been considerable use of coal—if you care to call it that. There is an old coal mine over on the east side of Mount Diablo, which lies to eastward of the Contra Costa hills; and it was this mine which supplied fuel for many of the boats, especially on the San Joaquin River run. It had one big advantage—it was cheap. From other standpoints, it was pretty terrible; but it gave heat of a sort. They loaded it at what then was known as Black Diamond Landing, the community which began life as the "New York of the Pacific" and is now called Pittsburg. Southern Pacific river boats used coal which was only slightly better than the Mount Diablo product, and which was brought down from a mine near Coos Bay, Oregon; it was bunkered at Vallejo. Boats like the *Apache* and the *Modoc* required an average of twenty-two tons of coal for the round trip from San Francisco to Sacramento and return—roughly 250 miles. In the last days of coal burning, the Southern Pacific boats used a soul-crushing commodity known to the trade as "Wellington screenings," which, according to Laurence E. Fish, one of the veteran engineers, was largely sand and coal dust.

"If anyone found a piece as big as an egg," Fish sourly observes, "it was a big day."

It was not until after 1900 that the use of oil became general; the explosion of the *Julia* in 1888 had dealt the oil-burners a blow from which they did not recover for more than a decade. At the time of the *Julia* disaster, oil had been installed as the fuel in the ferry steamer *Oakland,* ex-*Chrysopolis,* and in the 40-pound-pressure car-ferry *Solano.* Both installations were speedily removed, and everyone went back to coal. While it was not the *Julia*'s oil which blew up, there are those who feel that her oil-burner was at least a contributing factor. They argue that oil produces a hotter fire than coal and that hence the old wrought-iron boilers were overheated and weakened by an actual burning out of their furnaces.

The first oil-burners were gravity-fed, with no atomizers; the oil merely dripped from a tube into a pan, where it burned. When the *Solano*'s original boilers were replaced in 1905, old-timers pointed out the openings where these tubes had been fitted. Natural, crude oil, just as it came from the wells, was the original oil fuel—at 35 cents a barrel. Forty years later they were paying $1.25 a barrel for fuel from which much of the more volatile, and hence more valuable, oils had been removed.

Auxiliary machinery was simple—feed pumps, air pumps, pumps for fire, bilges, sanitary systems, and, in the case of the surface-condensing jobs, circulators. Later refinements included steam steering gear and, eventually, steam-driven dynamos for electric lights. Here, incidentally, the river boats had it on the ferries; for the first electric lights in the Far Western steamboats were aboard the old *City of Stockton* in 1889; they were carbon-filament bulbs, with glass shades shaped like calla lilies. Dynamos were installed in the *Apache* and the *Modoc*—the "mail boats"— in 1898, the same year that the first of the ferries, the steel-hulled *Berkeley,* came out, with electricity aboard. For the most part, however, inland craft stuck with the kerosene lamps for a long while; a photograph of the *Oakland*'s cabin in 1903 shows the oil lamps still in place. Old records of the Southern Pacific show that there was a general trend toward electric lighting in 1905—in fact, it was not until that year that the *Solano,* then the world's largest ferry, discarded her oil lamps. When the side-wheeler *Ramona* was built for the San Diego–Coronado ferry run in 1903, her owners made a great to-do over the fact that she was equipped with electric lights. Yet her companion on the same run, the little old *Coronado,* used hanging oil lanterns in her cabins right up to the end of her days; she was sold to Hollywood during the Fabulous 'Twenties; later rebuilt as a replica of a pirate ship, she blew up in a "battle" during the filming of Sabatini's *Captain Blood.* Swinging lanterns, however, were less common than the ornamental brass cabin-lamps and the big, square, brass bulkhead-lanterns used in the engine rooms and cargo decks.

So much, in a brief way, for the machinery. Now let us leave the heat, the rumbling furnaces, and the distinctive pungency of warm cylinder oil, and go back on deck for a breath of fresh air.

Chapter XI

BEYOND THE HEAD OF NAVIGATION

*B*ACK ABOUT THE TIME of the Battle of Bull Run, faint rumbles began to come in to the California State Legislature that unless something were done about the El Dorado Street situation the voters around Stockton might become a bit irked about it—and there was an election coming on. It seems that Nature had put a tributary of the San Joaquin right across where the Stocktonians wanted to run their street. So the lawmakers dug down into the legislative sock and came up with $6,000, which was enough, in those days, to build a very fair bridge.

Just to show that their hearts were in the right place, the Senators and Assemblymen then solemnly declared—and the Governor signed it, which made it final—that the El Dorado Street bridge was the head of navigation, so far as the San Joaquin was concerned. However, in this they failed to take into account the fact that if a steamboat captain turned off to the right just before he hit Stockton, he could by-pass the city—bridge and all—and head into better than two hundred miles of navigable water, right into the center of an up-and-coming agricultural empire.

Navigation on the upper San Joaquin, as a matter of fact, had

The Southern Pacific river steamer *Navajo* under way

The second *Gold* began life as the barge *Fort Bragg*.

Farmers on the upper Sacramento were served by the *Colusa*.

The capstan helped to move cargo at the landing near Corning.

been going on for more than a decade at the time the bridge was built. When the little *Georgiana* left Stockton for the south on the afternoon of May 1, 1850, she opened up a service which in time extended as far up the river as to and beyond Firebaugh[1] in Fresno County. She spent that night tied up to a tree on the bank above San Joaquin City, her people wrapping themselves up in their blankets and getting a few winks of sleep now and then when not too busily engaged in batting mosquitoes the size of field mice. Came the dawn—not a bit too soon—and the *Georgiana* and her little company of adventurers got under way again. From the San Joaquin they turned off into the Tuolumne, and steamed majestically into Tuolumne City[2] a short time later. They had proved that it could be done, and on returning to Stockton the owner-master of the little steamboat announced to all and sundry that he would make weekly trips to Grayson City and to Tuolumne City —at least, during high water—and would time his departure so that he could pick up, at Stockton, passengers and cargo brought up from San Francisco in the *John A. Sutter.* Thus was born what undoubtedly was the first "feeder service" in the history of steamers of the Far West. Two years later, the *Erastus Corning* found the going on the San Francisco-Stockton run a bit too rugged—there were six others to compete with—and muscled in on the *Georgiana*'s trade, with a schedule calling for regular stops at Empire City "and all intermediate points." Apparently, two-boat service for the run was too much, and the up-river business was abandoned soon after, not to be resumed until about 1860. Then two Stockton jewelers — the Ling brothers — built a stern-wheeler called the *Christiana,* which ran to the up-river landings for a quarter of a century and for some time included Tuolumne City in her itin-

[1] The present town of Firebaugh was then Firebaugh's Ferry, which makes it easier to trace on early maps than, for instance, the bustling little metropolis of Tuleberg, whose inhabitants, nearly a century ago, wisely decided to re-name it Stockton.

[2] Today, farmers tilling the fertile land some nine miles southwest of the city of Modesto may turn up a few bricks—all that remains of Tuolumne City. More lasting was Hill's Ferry, near the mouth of the Stanislaus, which survives as the little community of Hilmar, populated to a large extent by Swedish farmers who needed more elbow room as the town of Turlock grew.

erary. The *Esmeralda*—later to play her part in the development of the Colorado River steamboat trade—and the *Visalia* were put on the run to landings south of Stockton, and shuttled back and forth for years, with truly imposing manifests of grain, hides, lumber, farm machinery, livestock, etc. With the aid of these river steamboats there was being opened one of the nation's richest agricultural areas. Also the river steamboats were supplying the mines and the military outposts. Empire City—there's nothing left of it today but the cemetery—a dozen miles up the Tuolumne, was the site of an Army supply depot; it was the jumping-off place for old Fort Tejon, far to the south. At points as far south as Fresno feed and other supplies for the Overland stages were handled by river boat.

Bancroft's Guide for Travelers by Railway, Stage and Steam Navigation in the Pacific States, a booklet with a title nearly as long as itself, lists, in its 1871 edition, the California Pacific Railroad steamers *Tulare* and *Empire City* as making regular trips to Empire City and Mumford, with the "Opposition Steamers," *Clara Crow* and *Harriett* scheduled for the run to the long-vanished river landing of Watson's Ferry, two hundred fifty miles to the south. As a matter of fact, you could go by steamer to Sycamore Point, more than twenty miles above Watson's, during the high-water period which lasted from January to July, and thus get to within shouting distance of the town of Fresno, which was then called Fresno City. The craft on this run bore a family resemblance to the Colorado River packets; in both cases the open boiler deck—inherited from the steamboats of the Deep South—was a form of construction dictated by the extreme summer heat. The *Tulare* was, incidentally, the first up-river boat to have regular staterooms, the earlier ones having gone in exclusively for deck passengers who provided their own blankets and curled up wherever they were the least likely to be stepped on during the night. The *Tulare* is, moreover, worthy of some note in that at one time she ran from San Francisco to Tuolumne City direct: Stockton was, for her, a mere intermediate stop.

Navigation on the Stanislaus started out with the little *Tuol-*

omne City, which Stephen Davis, of Stockton, built in 1868 for a modest $9,000. She was a 90-foot stern-wheeler, with engines by the old Globe Iron Works of Stockton, and was in service for many years, finally dropping out of the register by 1885. The Tuolumne and Stanislaus Navigation Company got her when they organized in 1876; the State Legislature authorized them not only to operate on the river but also—at their own expense—to clear away trees along the banks which might topple over on a steamboat's smokestack. They cleared the river, both of snags and of overhanging branches, as far up as Barneyville.

All of this, of course, was before the Friant Dam and other irrigation projects had so drained the San Joaquin of water that it was useless from the standpoint of dependable navigation above Stockton. Low water was, of course, a problem always; and summer and fall navigation had to be approached with caution. In fact, the first boats to Tuolumne City learned that, to their sorrow. The little *Georgiana* had given the promoters of the town ambitious ideas of the future, and great plans had been made. But the ensuing summer months brought lower water, and when a steamboat got herself badly hung up on their landing a few months later the river navigators turned their backs on the town. So, for that matter, did most of its inhabitants. There was no more water-borne commerce there until some ten years later, when promoters had sense enough to use shallower boats. Tuolumne City was then briefly revived. Eventually the major part of the town was picked up, house by house, and moved over to Modesto, river navigation being discontinued in 1871.

Unprofitable as steam navigation on the Tuolumne, Stanislaus, and upper Mokelumne may have proved to be as a long-range proposition, the upper San Joaquin was destined to serve the stern-wheelers—and the stern-wheelers to serve the territory traversed by the river—for many years. Up they went with seed, groceries, farm machinery, lumber, and fuel, to return with clean cargoes of sacked grain or smelling vilely from their loads of green hides, livestock on the hoof, and other noisome things. But it was not to last forever; little by little the river dwindled in size as the precious waters were diverted for irrigation; and to the *J. R. McDonald,* in 1906, went the distinction of being the last steamer to Firebaugh. Receding waters of the river left her stranded, and it took persuasion of no mean sort, over a period of several weeks, to argue irrigation officials into opening the gates of a dam and letting out enough water to float her shallow hull. She lost no time in getting back to Stockton—and that was that, so far as steamboating in Fresno County is concerned.

The *J. R. McDonald,* incidentally, was one of the few river boats to carry a "monkey rudder"—a Columbia River importation which, for some reason, was never widely adopted on the San Joaquin or the Sacramento. This rudder—or rudders—hung from the fan-tail, just abaft the wheel, and extended down only to the waterline. When the wheel was turning ahead, of course, it lifted up a good deal of water in its wake, and in this water the two blades of the "monkey rudder" got in their work. The assembly was controlled by the same rudder-lines which operated the regular double or triple rudder, which was forward of the wheel. At one time they rigged this gear on one of the steamers of the *Delta* class, but as it hung down a bit too low—and was, moreover, braced by ironwork which was submerged—it added about an hour to the time which she needed for the run to Sacramento, and it was soon abandoned. The device, however, was very handy for boats working the sharp bends in the upper river, where extreme maneuverability, especially in towing barges, was essential.

California Navigation and Improvement Company—familiarly the "See-en-an'-eye"—was a big factor in the development of San Joaquin Valley steamboating; the *J. R. McDonald,* the *A. C. Freese,* and the *Leader* were their up-river boats. The barges which they towed were, in common with the Sacramento barges, big flat scows with quadruple rudders, and were steered from a pilothouse built up on stilts like a country windmill tower so that the helmsman could see over the high deckload of potatoes, grain, onions, chicory, or whatever else they were hauling. When one of these strings of barges came along, the bridge-tenders really had to be on their toes, for there was no stopping the steamer and her train of barges when they were heading downstream—if the draw did not open in time, the whole affair would pile up in a sorry mess. This was a hazard which made bridge permits hard to get and which kept the Delta isolated, so far as roads were concerned, for many years. Many of the big islands in the Delta region had no connection with the outside world except by steamboat for a long time. "See-en-an'-eye" also operated the *Mary Garrett,* the *J. D. Peters,* and others famous along the San Joaquin, and owned a big shipyard at Stockton, which was one of the main reasons why Sacramento Transportation Company was so anxious to buy them out in later years.

Mention has already been made of the possibility of getting from the San Joaquin over into the Sacramento without getting into salt water; and there was, in fact, a certain amount of business both in cargo and passengers between Stockton and Sacramento via Georgiana Slough; the first "liner" to make this trip was the *Gypsy,* which proudly steamed up to the landing at Sacramento and unloaded ten passengers direct from Stockton. It was possible, at high water stages, for a steamboat to leave Sycamore, make the 272-mile run down the San Joaquin to Stockton, cut across the lower Mokelumne and Georgiana Slough for roughly another 60 miles up to Sacramento, and then wind up with a run of 270 miles up to Red Bluff. She would thus have made a bit more than six hundred miles on fresh water, through the heart of California.

Navigation of the upper Sacramento was a going business as far back as 1850, when the stern-wheelers established a terminus at Moon House, near Corning, and then pushed on to Red Bluff, the head of navigation.[3] And, as always is the case, its history records the rugged individualist who had his own private ideas about how a steamboat should be built; here it was Dr. Robert Semple, who took time out from the practice of medicine to startle the world with a little homemade steamboat which we are told was named the *Colusa.* This noble venture lasted for just one voy-

[3] The first master of a regular up-river steamboat is reputed to have been Peter Lassen, for whom Mount Lassen, California's only active volcano, is named; he had the *Lady Washington.*

age; then she went back to San Francisco, where she discreetly dropped from view. Decay, marine borers, Bay pirates—today no one knows just what agency brought her to her end; at all events her life was not long enough to get her into any official listing of vessels or into published steamer schedules. Another up-river boat of the period—name not a matter of record—was snagged in the vicinity of Chico but carried on bravely ashore in later years, her salvaged timbers being used to build a hotel at Monroeville. For the next three years the *Orient* was a consistent performer on the upper Sacramento, going as far as Red Bluff when commercial inducements and depth of water were sufficient. Over a considerable period, steamboats carried the bulk of the business in passengers, cargo, and mails to the up-river communities, the trade gradually falling off as the railroad took over. Another early practitioner who left his name in river annals was Dr. Hugh J. Glenn, who started raising wheat in the northern valleys in 1867 and thereby supplied the steamboats with profitable down-river cargo. He also dealt in firewood, which was loaded on barges and floated down the Sacramento with the current, the tow back up the river being effected by the vessels of the California Steam Navigation Company, at rates which were attractive to the steamboat owners if not to their customers.

In the early 'sixties, Captain Thomas Dwyer decided to take a hand in river enterprise, and founded the Sacramento Wood Company, of which he was president and Captain J. H. Roberts was secretary. Theirs was, originally, strictly a barge-line business; but so unmercifully were they gouged by the steamboat people in the matter of up-stream towage bills that they decided to have their own motive power, and acquired their first vessel—the original *San Joaquin*. They built the *Varuna* in 1873 in their own yard at Broderick, over on the Yolo County side of the river, just across from Sacramento. She cost $50,000, and could carry 800 tons of cargo herself. In 1882 they renamed their concern the Sacramento Transportation Company,[4] which is still in existence; later on,

---

[4] For some obscure reason, in bygone years, this concern was known to rivermen as "The Dutch Company."

they bought out California Navigation and Improvement Company, lock, stock, and barrel, and thus became identified with river traffic on the San Joaquin as well as the Sacramento. In the up-river trade, they maintained regular service all the way up to Red Bluff as late as 1916. At that time they had seven steamers and twenty-three barges in the grain trade between the upper Sacramento and San Francisco Bay.

Another colorful name on a river which boasted such intriguing titles as Poker Bend, Sam Soule's Landing, and Gazelle Shoot was Squaw House, the landing for the town of Corning. It got its name from a shack occupied by two aged squaws whose braves had long since passed on to the Happy Hunting Grounds. The steamboat line built a sizable freight shed there, and it played its part in the commerce of the Sacramento from 1875 until 1910, when the last steamboat stopped there. Like so many other landings, Squaw House today is but a memory.

In 1874, Miller and Eaton put two steamers into service on the upper river; two others were provided for a weekly service on the Feather River, by E. D. Knight, N. D. Rideout, and W. T. Ellis of Marysville. In the following year the California Transportation Company came into being, with Captain A. Nelson as president and Captain N. Anderson as second in command. The first steamer built for their account was the original *Reform,* which came out in 1877 and lasted about ten years.

A name of importance in the up-river trade was that of the Farmers' Transportation Company, an opposition line established in 1901, when it put the *Valletta* in service on the Colusa run. Sacramento Transportation Company met this threat by increasing its own up-river service, and the rivals kept at it for a number of years. In 1914 the Farmers' outfit built the *Sacramento* (No. 4) for the northern run, and again "The Dutch Company" met the challenge. For something like a year Colusa thus had four weekly steamers to and from San Francisco, each line having two on the run. As this deal was doing neither line any great good financially, the competitors reached a gentlemen's agreement in 1917 and each took off a boat. In 1920 the two rival lines unified their operations under a separate corporation, the Sacramento Navigation Company.

The big consolidation took place in 1932, when Sacramento Navigation Company, California Navigation Company, and Fay Transportation Company—an up-and-going organization which had gone in heavily for Diesel boats—got together under the operating organization known as The River Lines. W. P. Dwyer, son of the founder of Sacramento Transportation, was named its president. When the days of steamboating were ended, they continued to run Diesels, and later trucks; today you will find California Navigation Company crockery being used by the officers and men of the motor vessel *San Joaquin,* nee *Dauntless* of 1892. You also will find one of her original, round-topped doors—a truly Victorian touch—leading into what now is the master's stateroom but over which appears the original white china plate dating back to her passenger-carrying days and bearing the legend, "Barber Shop."

No description of the up-river service would be complete without at least a passing mention of the trading boats *Sentinel, Neponset No. 2, Alvarado,* and *Weitchpec,* to name the more prominent ones. And just what, you may ask, was a trading boat? Well— she was in reality a floating general store, and you could go aboard and buy a tin lantern or a flitch of bacon, a bucket of axle grease or a set of long-handled underwear. Moreover, if you were short on cash, they would accept as payment a live hog or a sack of grain or a few lugs of potatoes, depending upon the value of your purchase. Incidentally, the rounding up of livestock for the river boats was something worth watching in itself, for cattle and hogs at the more isolated farms were nothing if not wild and were almost sure to be completely lacking in enthusiasm for boarding a steamboat. It took both force and cunning on the part of everyone—including the mates and deck hands—to get them aboard. This simple form of barter went on for a long time, the owner-captain of the boat being, if he remained long in business, a competent trader. The *Alvarado* seemed to go in for hogs on the hoof as her form of legal tender; hence, instead of stopping at San Francisco's more genteel wharves, she would paddle along down to Butcher Town to unload; at that point, the reek of her grunting, squealing cargo passed unnoticed amid the medley of foul odors already present. Having unloaded, all hands would turn to with fire hoses, and by the time she got back to San Francisco she was in condition to take on cargo of a less whiffy nature.

The *Weitchpec,* previously mentioned, was one of the few stern-wheelers to wear a hood over her paddle wheel; practically unknown until *Delta Queen* and *Delta King* came out, the hood was far more characteristic of the Columbia River than of the rivers of California. The *Weitchpec* was built at Fairhaven (later renamed Rolph) on Humboldt Bay, and before coming to the Sacramento ran between Eureka and Arcata. Perhaps the fact that she was built not too far from the California-Oregon line explains her possession of that distinctly Oregonian touch of naval architecture.

And that about covers the navigation of the upper rivers, albeit a bit briefly and purely from the standpoint of staying within the banks of the streams. There was another phase of river navigation which affected not only the upper reaches but the deeper parts as well—a phase which, for want of a better term, may be called wheat-field navigation. This was possible only at times of extreme high water, or during floods, when the resourceful pilot made good use of his knowledge that at a certain point a twelve-foot flood made Miguel Gonzalez' wheat field navigable or permitted one to cut across Hop Chong's potato patch. So, cut across those fields they did, at least in the shallower stern-wheelers. During the big flood of 1861–62, we are told, steamers went from Stockton to Sacramento by a somewhat direct route, traveling over fields and meadows where their navigating marks were tall trees, or the chimneys of farmhouses, surrounded by swirling, muddy water.

There are no records of steamers being wrecked on shingled roofs, so it must have worked.

CHAPTER XII

"YOU GET OFF HERE, MISTER"

THERE WERE literally hundreds of landings on the Sacramento and the San Joaquin during the later days of steamboating—landings, in fact, where a boat would stop for as little cargo as a lug of peaches.

Modern charts of the rivers still show, in addition to the named landings, many which were merely numbered. What probably is the record for the number of stops to lift merchandise was a run by the *Isleton* shortly after the turn of the century; on one trip she made forty-six landings on her way from San Francisco up to Sacramento, and touched at seventy-six on her way back down-river. Most of those landings are gone now; sheds have been pulled down or have collapsed, and of the landings themselves little remains.

Many of the stops, especially on the Sacramento, were made at what were known as "brush landings"—that is, instead of being wharves, they were merely masses of brush, fruit-tree prunings, asparagus roots, and similar waste, dumped into the water at the river's edge. A steamboat would nose up to one of these landings, swing out her gangplank, lay planks across the brush, and trundle cargo aboard or ashore with hand trucks; sometimes, if the cargo offering consisted only of a lug or so of vegetables or fruit, the deck hands would merely toss it up on their shoulders and trot aboard. The engineer, while this was going on, was as important as the pilot. Looking out through the engine-room windows to judge his position, he would handle the throttle with such nicety—and without any bells from the pilot—that he kept her in just the right position, without the use of mooring lines, until cargo operations were completed. He was a peaceful counterpart—without the accompanying holocaust—of the legendary and heroic Jim Bludso, who swore to "hold her nozzle agin the bank 'till the last galoot's ashore!"

If a farmer had cargo for a Southern Pacific boat he would hang out a white flag by day, a white lantern by night. If his cargo, on the other hand, were intended for a member of Sacramento Transportation's fleet, he indicated it by displaying a red flag or a red lantern to call in the passing steamboat. The same signals would get you passage for yourself and your hand luggage.

Before the advent of buses, ranch hands destined for river points traveled chiefly by boat. Many of these farm laborers were Chinese, and the mates of the steamers grew old before their time trying to figure just where to stop for an Oriental who could not speak enough English to make his destination known. Finally, the operators hit upon the scheme of putting Chinese "runners" aboard the boats, and this task became simpler. The mate would tell the runner that they were approaching, let us say, Paintersville. The runner would then round up the clients for that community, and they would all be out on deck and ready to go when the boat came alongside the landing.

For the isolated farm landings, the routine was a bit more

rugged. If there was but one passenger, and he a farm hand or a bindle stiff, the mate would have the gangway rigged out as they came up to a brush landing which served whatever farm he desired. Then—"You get off here, mister"—and the unsuspecting passenger would be motioned out onto the gangway. Close behind him, and politely carrying his suitcase or bedroll, would be a deck hand—a big one. The passenger, seeing that there was nothing on which to step but the uninviting mass of brush, would try to get back; this was where the deck hand came in. A large foot, planted in the seat of the victim's pants, was all that was needed. Over he went, frequently to disappear to his armpits in the brush. His luggage was tossed after him, and the boat went on about its business.

But it was good service—so good, in fact, that the farmers rode it to death. As operating costs slowly rose, it became more and more apparent that this business of stopping for a basket of peaches at one landing and for a crate of asparagus at one a hundred yards farther on would have to stop. For this reason, the operators ruled that no steamer would stop for less than $1.25 worth of business. Although this idea was financially sound, it was resented by the farmers, who were not slow to turn to the truck concerns. The latter lost no time in selling the agriculturists the idea that it was better to have the trucks come right into their fields and pick up the cargo for San Francisco direct than it was to cart it along to the next landing to meet the tariff requirement. That was, generally speaking, the end of the pick-up trade along the river.

Along the San Joaquin there were fewer stops, and most of the tonnage among the Delta islands was on the basis of carload or two-carload lots; there was little of what is known to the trade as "LCL," or "less than carload lots." Among these islands the Chinese grew potatoes, the Italians specialized in beans, and the Japs went in for onions in a big way. A stop at a potato landing was always an adventure. The steamer would come in, perhaps in the middle of the night, and find not a living soul in sight. Muttering his opinion of farmers in general and potato-growers in particular, the pilot would yank lustily on the whistle-pull. If this brought no results, the vessel's officers would go over the side and head for the bunkhouse, pounding on the door and shouting until they got an answer and a string of sleepy and half-clad Chinese came out.

At these farms the Chinese all worked on a partnership basis, and the final settling of the cargo tally was not without discussion. Some would be checking off the sacks of potatoes by marks scratched in the dust with a stick; others, more advanced in learning, would be busy with the abacus, and the pilot and mate of the steamer would be making their own count at the same time. No two of the farmers ever came up with the same answer; but the minute any one of them agreed with the figure arrived at by the freighter's officers the rest of the crew would brush the gesticulating Orientals aside and start bringing the potato sacks aboard. When the job was done, the steamer took in her plank, backed out into the slough, and with a cheery toot from her whistle, went on to the next stop, leaving the consignors of her cargo to argue it out among themselves.

All this time improvements were being made in the river passenger vessels. The *Fort Sutter* and the *Capital City* startled the world by coming out with staterooms which had private baths; they may have caused no great ripple of excitement among the bindle-stiff clientele, who were allergic to soap anyhow; but the innovation immediately caught the fancy of the more polite travelers topside, and these boats got the cream of the business until the huge *Delta King* and *Delta Queen* came out.

Along in the 'nineties the Union Transportation Company operated the *Dauntless* and the *Captain Weber* on the Stockton run. Mrs. Sarah Gillis, a leader in the Stockton local of the W.C.T.U., became a controlling factor in this line upon the death of her husband, who had been its president. As a result, these two were the only dry steamers on the rivers, all of the rest being equipped with well-stocked "buffets," as they called them in those days; the modern appellation of "cocktail lounge" for a blacked-out saloon in which anything can happen was a pitfall of civilization yet to come. The *Captain Weber* was considered the fastest of the Stockton boats, and indeed her hull lines were nothing if not sweet. Her only rival in speed was the two-stacker *H. J. Corcoran,* which later was to achieve wide publicity by mortally wounding the *Seminole* when she crashed into her during a dense fog near Angel Island in 1913. Later, the California Transportation Company bought out the Union Line and the *Captain Weber* was rebuilt. Had Mrs. Gillis lived to see it, she would have been a most unhappy lady indeed; for the first thing the new owners did was to put in a bar. However, they made another improvement of which no one could complain—they widened the vessel's dining room to the entire width of the cabin. Previously the river steamers' dining rooms had been tunnels down the center of the deckhouses from which you could see nothing but the doors of the staterooms. The new idea caught on at once; the *Captain Weber* got the pick of the passenger trade; and, as new vessels were built or old ones overhauled, the dining room with a view came in.

In their later years the steamboats ran at night; you left San Francisco about six o'clock in the evening, and were at Sacramento or at Stockton in the morning with the whole day before you; then, back aboard as night approached, you returned to "The City" by morning. For the majority of travelers it was a straight business proposition, plus rest and relaxation en route. For others a night trip on the river boats was an adventure—and you may interpret that remark in any way you choose. While it would be grossly unfair to characterize the night boat as a floating bagnio, there frequently were among the more playful passengers those who, let us say, looked upon the proprieties with perhaps undue breadth of mind. It was not always safe, therefore, to assume that the charming companion of Mr. X was, in fact, Mrs. X. Regarded with much more alarm by the crew members of the steamboats were large groups bound en masse for a convention or a football game, or—worst of all—an excursion of flaming youth of high-school age. They were the ones who gave the mates and pursers and stewards a need for aspirin in case lots and made replacements for pilferage and broken windows a real item in operating costs.

As respects conventions, the river-boat people may have had in mind what the Emmett Guards did to the poor old *Chrysopolis,* when some nameless saboteur suggested, in 1891, an excursion up to Sacramento to see that Governor H. H. Markham was properly inaugurated. For then the celebrators—a crowd of several hundred San Francisco politicos and hangers-on, accompanied by a brass band, a more than ample supply of hard liquor, and a small cannon—wound up by making the voyage in the ferryboat *Bay City.* She got them to the state capitol in fair shape, their arrival at a point below the old M Street bridge[1] being announced by the booming of the cannon and by band music which was neither too good nor outstandingly bad. At the conclusion of the day's ceremonies the San Francisco delegates either walked or were carried back aboard the *Bay City,* and were off for home. It is not recorded that they did the fine old double-ender any lasting harm, for she continued to serve the commuters of San Francisco Bay for many years afterward.

A variation from the almost universal custom of running the river boats at night was furnished by the Southern Pacific's veteran *Apache* and *Modoc,* which, about 1912 and for several years thereafter, left San Francisco and Sacramento in the morning. Incidentally, the company made use of the annual Fourth of July picnic at Rio Vista to give the crews of these boats a bit of a change. Normally, of course, the boat which left San Francisco on Tuesday, Thursday, and Saturday would continue to do so indefinitely, and her week-end layover always would be at Sacramento. To vary this monotony, the boat leaving Sacramento on the morning of July 4 stopped at Rio Vista, where she met the up-boat from San Francisco; after the picnic, she doubled back to Sacramento with the returning picnickers, while her through passengers went on to San Francisco in the other boat. Thus the two schedules were reversed. Two other well-known Southern Pacific boats were the *Navajo,* which came out in 1909, and the *Seminole,* which followed her two years later; both were night boats, and these two

[1] A Gargantuan lift-bridge of modernistic architecture now marks the spot. And M Street has gone up-stage, too; it is now called Capitol Avenue.

comfortable and well-appointed craft were in service until the rail-road line went out of the river-passenger business, about 1918.

While the river boats had their lighter moments, and there may have been occasional strayings from the straight and narrow path by some of their customers, there were, for the boats and their own people, more than enough of outstanding virtues—friendly co-operation, absolute honesty, and famous meals, to name but a few. Up-river banks shipped thousands of dollars in gold to San Francisco, in little iron boxes. At times, these precious bits of cargo would lie for hours on a wharf, completely unguarded. Everyone knew what the boxes contained—but none of them was ever touched. Just try that sort of thing today and see what happens. And characteristic of the little things which the steamer people did for their customers was the service of Johnny Myrick, one of the famous pilots. Sacramento housewives, unable themselves to get to San Francisco, would make out shopping lists and hand them to Myrick, together with the funds necessary for their purchases. The spectacle of a hard-boiled river pilot buying corsets or other feminine impedimenta in San Francisco stores no doubt brought raised eyebrows among those who did not know what was going on; but he didn't mind. Had he charged for his services in this trade—which he did not—he could have made a neat little sum on the side. It is small wonder that the name of the kindly and obliging pilot is remembered on the river to this day.

As Chinese living along the rivers died, it was customary, when-ever possible, to send the bodies back to China for burial. A certain amount of down-river tonnage to San Francisco hence con-sisted of the grim pine boxes in which the caskets were encased for the long voyage home. Down-to-earth dock clerks, however, were unimpressed by the solemnity of the occasion; some would stand with one foot on the box while making out bills of lading, while others found them handy places on which to sit during the lunch hour. But then—you'll find that sort of thing anywhere.

Chapter XIII

DEEP BENEATH LAKE MEAD

YOU CAN'T TAKE a steamboat from Yuma up to Callville, Nevada, any more; in the first place, there are no such craft left on the Colorado, and, in the second place, there are dams across the river for collecting irrigation water. And it wouldn't do you any good, even if you could get there; for Callville long ago became a mere heap of tumbled adobe ruins. To make it final, that picturesque settlement was just a bit upstream from the site of Boulder Dam, and it now lies beneath several hundred feet of the waters of Lake Mead.

Perhaps it is a bit far-fetched to include Colorado River navigation in a chronicle of the California river steamers—and then perhaps it is not. At any event, the Colorado, for quite a bit of its length, forms the eastern boundary of California, and hence a part of its navigation is as much a proper subject for discussion under the heading of California history as it would be under that of Arizona[1] or of Nevada. Moreover, Yuma, headquarters for

[1] This idea, in bygone years, no doubt would have aroused a bit of caustic comment from Yuma's hardy old *Arizona Sentinel,* which from time to time hinted that its contemporary, the *San Diego Union,* would do well to keep its nose in its own affairs and stop criticizing things as they were being run in the Arizona Territory.

river navigation, has not always been exclusively in Arizona; part of it at one time was in San Diego County, California, and several early steamboats and barges paid their taxes there. This odd situation developed about as follows: Under the terms of the Treaty of Guadalupe Hidalgo, the boundary between the United States and Mexico was a line running from a point three marine leagues below the southerly tip of San Diego Bay, easterly to the confluence of the Colorado and Gila rivers. So far, so good. Now, after leaving the Gila, the Colorado does some fancy twisting and turning, to such an extent that it actually runs northwest—and hence inside of the San Diego–Gila line—for a short distance, in its attempt to go south into the Gulf of California. Therefore, several hundred acres of what now is Yuma lie to the north of the old boundary line. In those days there was no Imperial County; San Diego County ran all the way across the bottom of the state, and so Yuma was in San Diego County. San Diego was, moreover, the home port of the little river steamboat *General Jessup,* which never got closer to that seaport than some hundred and forty-five miles of mountain and desert.

It was in 1851, the year after Major Samuel Heintzelman established Fort Yuma to protect travelers from the Indians, that the Army gave Captain George A. Johnson a contract to transport freight from San Francisco to the sizzling territorial outpost and the first load came into the head of the Gulf in the schooner *Sierra Nevada;* it was transferred to flatboats which Johnson had built and which were poled up the river to Yuma. The first steamboat on the river was the diminutive *Uncle Sam,* a side-wheeler, which had been brought down from San Francisco in the hold of a schooner and re-assembled at the river's mouth; she reached Fort Yuma on December 29, 1852.[2] Little more than a sizable steam launch, she was 65 feet long and drew only 22 inches of water— about all that can be said in her favor is that she was the first of the Colorado River fleet. When she sank at her moorings at Pilot

---

[2] There is a legend that the *Uncle Sam* was preceded by a little stern-wheeler called the *Yuma,* which scared the Indians but did little else of value. No record of her, however, can be found.

Knob, a few miles down the river from Yuma, on June 22, 1854, they just left her there. Her owner-builder was a Captain Trumbull, of whom the following word-picture is handed down in the musty files of the *Sentinel:* "an energetic, smooth-talking little fellow, who afterward became well known around Mazatlan, where he ran a little stern-wheel boat for years; and better known for his attempts to build canals, etc., down there on pure jawbone —without any money at all."

The next steamboat to appear on the river was the *General Jessup,* also a side-wheeler. A coastwise windjammer brought her, sectionally, to the mouth of the Colorado; and she began running early in 1854. A bit more ambitious than her predecessor, she was 108 feet long, with a width of 28 feet over the guards, and she drew 30 inches of water. Captain Johnson, her owner, used her to carry north from Yuma such cargo as was offered, and also for towing barges up from the transfer point at Port Isabel, where the schooners unloaded, down near the mouth of the Colorado. Now only a memory, Port Isabel boasted a drydock and a machine shop, and was the place where several of the river boats were either erected or actually built. The drydock was something of a novelty itself, being entirely innocent of the pumps and similar impedimenta which generally are part of such an enterprise; it was merely a shallow basin scooped out of the sand, and lined with planks. Owing to the fact that there is a tidal range of twenty-two feet at the head of the Gulf of California, the job of filling and emptying the chamber of the little drydock on the Colorado Delta was simple. You merely left the dock gate open when the tide was out, and let the waters of the next flood-tide fill it. At the same time, you ran your barge or steamboat into the dock, and got it on the keel blocks as the water receded. Then the gate was closed, keeping out succeeding tides until the repair job was done, when the filling process was repeated and the steamboat serenely paddled away.

In 1853, Captain Johnson got together with Benjamin Hartshorne and a Captain Wilcox and founded the Colorado Steam Navigation Company. Cargo now began to move along the river in dead earnest. Not only was there tonnage to carry on the last leg of the voyage from San Francisco to Yuma but also troops, mining machinery, prospectors, and groceries to be taken to points far up the river. It was tricky navigation, for the stream altered so continually that this week's channel might well become next week's sand bar. Hence there was little if any navigation at night; and there was a great deal of sounding with poles, by the Cocopah Indian deck hands. In spite of this, some very fair runs were made; the *Cocopah* (No. 2) is credited with a 220-mile jaunt from an up-river camp down to Yuma in 1878 at a speed which was just a shade under twenty miles an hour.

The river had meanwhile been surveyed by the jovial Lieutenant Derby, who transferred its twists and turns and sand bars —as of that moment—to paper in 1852. The river's most famous survey, however, was to come some six years later, after the stream was already being used as a recognized artery of commerce.

The original *Colorado,* a stern-wheeler 120 feet in length, was built at the little shipyard down on the Delta in 1855, probably from prefabricated parts. A slim, sharp-bowed craft, she was held by some to have been the fastest steamer ever used on the river; and she served the Colorado Steam Navigation Company well until 1862, when she was dismantled and her machinery was used for the newer, larger *Colorado* (No. 2), built at Yuma the same year. It was, incidentally, the Civil War which caused her to be built at Yuma, rather than at Port Isabel. Her owners, it seems, were apprehensive that a Confederate raider might sneak up the Colorado and capture both the shipyards and the new steamer. Just what the Johnny Rebs would do with a river steamboat so far from the Deep South was not made clear, but such was the state of war jitters at the time that anything must have seemed possible. At any rate, the *Colorado* was built under the protection of Fort Yuma's guns. However, Port Isabel has a number of other vessels to its credit and can afford to get along in history without the timid *Colorado*. Vessels known to have been built completely at the little shipyard or assembled there from parts shipped down from San Francisco are the *General Jessup,* the *Cocopah* (No. 1), the

Cocopah (No. 2), the *Colorado* (No. 1), the *Mohave* (No. 1), the *Mohave* (No. 2), the *Gila,* and a number of barges. Data on these vessels are virtually nonexistent; under the free and easy procedure of those bygone days you just built yourself a steamboat, went around to the nearest customhouse and had her documented, and proceeded with your business; then after a time they cleaned out the customhouse records and had a nice bonfire. Another little oddity of the time is the fact that, although many of the stern-wheelers were actually built in Mexico, no import duty was paid on them. With a commendable spirit of co-operation, the customs officials eased their consciences in this manner: Yes, the boats were built in Mexico—but the lumber from which they were built had been shipped in from the United States, and they had been built with American money. That made them American-built vessels, didn't it?

The little *General Jessup* was not destined to make old bones, but at least she carved herself a niche in history. Arriving on the river in January 1854, she was the first steamboat ever to go above Yuma. In August of the same year she sank, after hitting a rock near Picacho. They raised her, and she is reported to have actually gone later as far up the Colorado as Black Canyon, the present site of Boulder Dam. In 1859 she gave the Colorado its only steamboat explosion of which a record can be found—she blew up while at her landing, and killed one of her crew.

It was shortly before this that the government decided upon another survey of the Colorado, with the definite object of proving or disproving its availability for the purposes of navigation. And, although the Johnson outfit already had steamboats on the river, it was decided for some reason[3] that they would not serve and that a special craft would have to be built, just for the job. The resulting maritime monstrosity was an iron-hulled affair called the *Explorer,* built in the East, shipped out in pieces, and re-assembled at Yuma. It is hard to describe the *Explorer,* for she was unlike anything afloat at that time, at any previous time, or, it is to be hoped, at

[3] An inclination, on various occasions, to gig poor old Uncle Sam to the tune of $500 a day for steamboat hire may have had something to do with this decision.

any future time. She was all open, with a high stern-wheel and a pulpit-like arrangement for the pilot far aft. And she was only fifty feet in length.

With Lieutenant Joseph C. Ives, U.S.A., in command, the little party left Fort Yuma on January 11, 1858, heading up the river. It took them until March 12 to get through Black Canyon, a matter of some three hundred miles; and it must have been quite a trip. At one point they hit a rock and bashed in the poor little *Explorer*'s nose. In what must have been a minor classic of what we now call Damage Control, they got her fixed up and went on their way, finally reaching the mouth of the Virgin River, away up in Nevada. All the while, we can imagine that they were not too well pleased by their reception at the hands of the local citizenry —which consisted exclusively of aborigines in what today would be called a shocking state of deshabille. The noble redskins trotted happily along the bank of the river; whenever the *Explorer* found a new mudbank, by the simple expedient of getting hung up on it, they would burst into gales of coarse laughter. This seems in time to have got on the nerves of the *Explorer*'s people, as well it might. Not only is it unpleasant at best to be twitted by local hoodlums but in those days you never could tell when an Indian would decide that he was tired of the joke and would have at you with an assortment of sharp and blunt implements. At any rate, Lieutenant Ives, on his return to civilization, wrote an official report in which he hinted that so far as he was concerned the Colorado was no decent place for navigation. This cynical outlook may have been aggravated by the fact that as he returned down river, after many vicissitudes, he met one of Johnson's regular steamers going up. The Johnsonites made a bad matter worse by appearing to be mildly amused. That is about all there is to the history of the little *Explorer*. As she was a misfit and nobody wanted her, they tied her up to a tree—and one night the Colorado, as was its custom, grew tired of its old course and decided to move over a bit. The tree tumbled into the river and floated off, as did the *Explorer*. That was the last that anyone saw of her—or at least, so they thought at the time. But that is getting ahead of the story.

Meanwhile, there had been other developments. Along about 1864 Captain Thomas E. Trueworthy, who owned a big barge on the Sacramento, decided to get into the lucrative trade to Arizona Territory. So he had the barge stiffened a bit, rigged it as a four-masted schooner—probably the world's first vessel of this rig—and into her he loaded 450,000 board feet of lumber. He called the thing the *Victoria,* and set sail from San Francisco for Port Isabel. From San Francisco to Cape San Lucas is downhill all the way, in the matter of both wind and current; so they made it all right. Then they beat their way up the Gulf of California into the tortuous mouth of the Colorado and let go their anchor off Port Isabel. Apparently the great rise and fall of the tide was not taken into consideration, for on the next ebb the hapless *Victoria* sat down on the up-turned fluke of her own anchor, and holed herself pretty badly. The next few tidal "bores" of the Colorado did the rest, and there was lumber scattered all over the Delta. But her people got off safely—including a young A.B. named Jack Mellen. He decided that he would stay with the river, and stay with it he did, becoming one of the Colorado's most famous pilots and at last proud master of the river's biggest steamboat, the impressive two-stacker *Mohave,* which was built in 1876 and lasted for nearly a quarter of a century.

No river steamboat company ever existed for long, or made any amount of money, without having someone start up an opposition line, and the Colorado was no exception. Shortly after the *Victoria* debacle, Captain Trueworthy again appeared on the river, this time with the *Esmeralda,* late of the Stockton–San Francisco run. Not only did she make the trip all the way down the coast and up into the Gulf on her own steam, but at Yuma she picked up a barge and went right on, up to Callville, then a cargo-receiving point for the Mormon colony in southern Utah. Simultaneously the Philadelphia Mining Company brought out the *Nina Tilden,* and the two independent boats put up real competition for the wicked monopoly. At the end of a year the owners of the two boats found an optimistic soul who was willing to buy, and sold out. The new owner had but little better luck than the original ones, and in 1867 Colorado Steam bought its erstwhile rival. That was the end of competition on the river. The *Esmeralda* had vanished from the *List of Merchant Vessels* by 1868; the *Nina Tilden* was not long in following her, and her demise was not without incident. The tidal "bore" of the Colorado, already mentioned, is a perilous thing; on the flood tide the flowing waters of the river meet the incoming ones from the Gulf to form a high wall of water which moves up the river with no mean force —which is not strange when one considers that 22-foot range of tide. One night in 1874 when the *Nina Tilden* was moored in the channel at Port Isabel her bow-line parted, her bow drifted out into the river, and the oncoming bore caught her and rolled her over, carrying away all of her upper works. During succeeding low tides her owners chopped away her bottom and took out her boilers and engines, leaving the shattered hull to drift away as it willed.

The transfer of the *Esmeralda* was not the only case of an interchange of equipment between the Colorado and the San Joaquin or the Sacramento. On the other side of the ledger, we have the case of the engines from the original *Cocopah*, which were taken out when she was dismantled in 1872 and sent north for the *Hattie Fickett*, then building for the Stockton run; also the engines from the first *Mohave*, dismantled in 1874, which three years later were placed in the *Onward*, to drive her to and from the river ports above San Francisco until around 1909.

Colorado steamboats were of typically Western design, much like the stern-wheelers used in later years on the rivers emptying into San Francisco Bay. They were flat-bottomed, and the boiler deck was entirely open, its forward part being used for cargo. On the upper deck there were staterooms—of a sort—and the galley and the dining room were located there also. Travel in these boats was something which was undertaken from necessity, generally speaking, and not for pleasure. Blistering heat, canned food, butter which was reduced to a gooey mess, and frequent strandings on the shifting bars marred the daylight hours; at night mosquitoes descended in fiendish glee upon passengers and crew, who made it a point to try to get under cover as soon as it got dark, and the vessel was secured for the night. The river was, of course, innocent of any lighted navigational aids.

Callville petered out, as a town of any great importance, about 1869. In 1877 the Southern Pacific reached Yuma, and shortly afterward it bought out Colorado Steam. Port Isabel was abandoned in 1878 and, although river traffic from Yuma south to the Gulf of California was over, there continued to be quite a bit of trade to points to the north.

A little booklet whose cover is devoted almost entirely to its extensive title, *Crofutt's New Overland Tourist and Pacific Coast Guide for 1880,* gives us a hint as to what rates were charged on the river in those days. It lists the following: Yuma to Castle Dome, 35 miles, $5.00; to Ehrenberg, 125 miles, $15.00; to Aubry, 220 miles, $28.00; to Camp Mohave, 300 miles, or Hardyville, 312 miles, $35.00; and to El Dorado Canyon, a bit below Callville, and allegedly 365 miles from Yuma, $45.00. The distances, incidentally, should be accepted with some reserve: take a pair of dividers and step it off on the map, and you don't get the same answer at all. In some cases, they seem to have used the mileage from Port Isabel, and the error in distance—always on the side of the steamboat people—sometimes was a hundred miles or more. Freight was $47.50 a ton from San Francisco to Yuma by schooner and steamboat, and $77.50 a ton to Fort Mohave. On the other hand, you could ship ore from Ehrenberg to San Francisco for $15.00 a ton—less than a third of the rate on general cargo from San Francisco to Yuma; one is inclined to suspect that the mining people and the steamboat people were very good friends indeed. At the time when this schedule was published, steamers left Yuma each week for Aubry, at the mouth of Bill Williams' River, from the first Saturday in May until the end of October; then it dropped to every second Saturday for the rest of the year. Beginning in mid-January, there was a boat every fifth Wednesday to Camp Mohave, while intermittent service was maintained from May 1 to the last of October as far up as El Dorado Canyon, height of water permitting.

Mining machinery, provisions, and general merchandise made

up the bulk of the up-river trade, while ore provided most of the down-stream tonnage. Passengers were chiefly miners, or soldiers bound to or for the various outposts. It was rugged voyaging, and the tariff presents an interesting contrast to that of the big *Delta* boats on the Sacramento. There, traveling in comfort if not in downright luxury, you could make a run about as long as that from Yuma to Ehrenberg for comfortably less than $10.00, including your fare, stateroom, superb meals, and the transportation of your automobile on the cargo deck below.

There still were fair-sized steamboats on the Colorado at the turn of the century. The *Mohave* occasionally shifted over from the role of freighter to that of excursion boat, making short runs with crowds of picnickers aboard, and others found a bit of tonnage here and there. But the backbone of the river business had been broken by rail competition, leaving only local or feeder trade for the steamers; an irrigation dam across the river ended it, once and for all, in 1908. The little *Searchlight,* built in 1903, was the last stern-wheeler to be launched on the river, and by 1909 she had disappeared from the shipping lists, as had the steel-hulled *St. Vallier,* built in 1899.

So ends a brief sketch of steamboating on that important stream, a subject on which, if all the yarns were dug up, much more could be written. Today there are many who are frankly surprised to learn that there ever were steamboats on the river which traverses not only the shimmering sands of the desert but also some of the most astoundingly magnificent scenery in the world. It was a distinct surprise, for instance, to the members of a survey party who in 1930 trudged along one of the river's long-abandoned courses some thirty miles southwesterly from Yuma, when they came upon a big, flat pan of rusting iron plates. It dawned upon them that they were looking at what once had been the hull of a steamboat; there it lay, forlorn and alone, in a meander of the river which long since had gone dry as the stream had cut itself a new course through the soft earth.

Yes, it was a steamboat, all right. It was the forgotten hull of Lieutenant Ives's poor little *Explorer.*

Chapter XIV

"THE BOATS ARE ALL ON FIRE!"

$\mathscr{A}$ FOUR-ALARM BLAZE at the head of Stockton Channel on the pleasant Saturday afternoon of May 22, 1943, was more than a mere source of free entertainment for the idle. It was a fire which threatened wharves and buildings along Stockton's water front; it called out all of the city's available fire apparatus, plus a Coast Guard fireboat and the wartime auxiliary firemen, before the flames were quenched. And with it there passed into history the last of California's river steamboats of the Victorian era, the grand old *Captain Weber;* its cold and sodden hulk later was towed away to Rio Vista, there to be converted into an elevator barge.

Not only had the *Captain Weber* served commerce faithfully during her life span of more than half a century but she was known to millions of people throughout the world who, although they had never been near a California river, had seen her in the motion pictures *Steamboat Round the Bend,* with the immortal Will Rogers, and *Dixie,* where she co-starred in a modest way with Bing Crosby. California's streams made a convenient location for cinema producers engaged in turning out river stories;[1] these, however, were always stories of the Mississippi or the Ohio and never dealt with the colorful past of the Sacramento, the San Joaquin, or the Colorado. *Dixie* depicted, among other things, two theater fires and the burning of a stately Southern mansion, but showed no steamboat fires; that came later in the career of the film's most costly "prop." There was an earlier picture, incidentally, which featured a steamboat disaster displaying what is said to have been far greater realism than was intended. That was away back in 1916, at Wood Island, when they were working on *Jim Bludso.* The stern-wheeler *Grace Barton,* built in 1890 for the San Francisco–Vallejo run, was used for that thriller of the silent films and, according to old-timers, her destruction by fire was not intentional. It seems that something went wrong with the smoke pots, and the first thing they knew the *Grace Barton* was on fire. The extreme realism which marked the flight of her "passengers" was the result of dire necessity rather than of superb directing.

When the *Captain Weber* burned she still was rigged with the flaring crowns on her stacks, the plywood gingerbread work, and the white stern-wheel — vermilion was the traditional color — which had disguised her as the *Cumberland* in *Dixie.* And it was while working on what was destined to be her final picture that she had the distinction of being the last of the once huge fleet of stern-wheel steamboats to make the winding trip from tidewater up to Sacramento.[2]

Most of the river fires occurred while the steamers were alongside the wharves at night, were temporarily out of service, or had already been abandoned. If such a fire went undiscovered long

---

[1] These included *Jim Bludso,* released in 1917; *Steamboat Round the Bend,* 1928; *Huckleberry Finn,* 1931; and *Dixie,* 1943.

[2] The last side-wheeler up to Sacramento, veteran rivermen say, was the *Amador,* which took troops up from San Francisco at the time of the big railroad strike in 1892.

enough to get any headway at all, the situation generally was hope-
less. Wooden hulls, wooden decks, wooden cabins which were of
necessity fairly well ventilated—all contributed to such an outcome. Even the paddle wheels were of wood, except for the axles
and hubs; the spokes were of oak or apatong, and the buckets
were vertical-grain Oregon pine. Many coats of paint—not count-
ing the landscapes done in oil on the panels, by such well-known
California artists as William Keith or Albert Bierstadt—provided
additional fuel. In the beginning, even the hog-framing, which
acted as a truss to give the hull its longitudinal strength and to
prevent hogging or sagging, was of wood, although in the later
steamers only the hog-posts themselves were timbers, steel rods
and turnbuckles being provided where there was tension. Such
construction, well dried out by the summer heat of the Sacramento
or the San Joaquin Valley, will burn like tinder once it is fairly
alight, as any municipal fireman will tell you. Small wonder that
alert watchmen were always prowling around when the boats
were under way, or that fire-pumps, extinguishers, axes—and even,
in some cases, automatic sprinklers—were liberally supplied. For
in spite of the almost universally wooden construction, precau-
tionary measures were such that passengers had little to fear in
the matter of fire.

No published statistics on the loss of merchant vessels before
1906 exist, and thus it is difficult at this late day to say just how
many burned before that time. If a vessel had been abandoned
before her burning, there was no record of it even then. It was not
until 1921 that the authorities began to list vessels abandoned, sold
alien, reduced in tonnage, or otherwise disposed of by nonviolent
means. The best of official records give only the date and place of
burning, the number of persons aboard, and how many lives—if
any—were lost. For anything else, including the basic fact of
the burning of an abandoned steamer, we must fall back on the
memories of the old-timers who can recall the incidents. Even in
official listings the dates may be wrong.[3] We must be content with

---

[3] This was by no means exclusively the fault of those who compiled the records.
Sometimes the owners of a vessel might delay in surrendering her document to

knowing, for example, that the *F. M. Smith* went up in flames on the Alameda mud flats, with one man aboard when the fire broke out and with no lives lost, on May 30, 1909. A more serious fire was the burning, about a year later, of the *San Joaquin No. 3.* She was all loaded with cargo at Sacramento, ready to head up-river for Chico with thirty-two persons aboard, on July 25, 1910. She caught fire as a result of a fuel-oil explosion; the flames spread with some rapidity, but only two injuries were reported.

The second *Petaluma*—ex-*Resolute*—caught fire as she lay at the wharf in Petaluma, also with a full cargo aboard, shortly after the engineer and watchman made their 3:00 A.M. inspection on March 22, 1914; spontaneous combustion in a big consignment of empty sacks was generally accepted as the cause; and, although the crew and passengers had to flee in whatever type of nocturnal garments they were wearing, no one was hurt. They cut her lines and shoved her out into the stream, thereby saving the wharf and warehouses; but all that could be salvaged from the vessel herself was the machinery, which was used in the third *Petaluma,* built immediately afterward.

There had been many changes in the social status of the old *Caroline* between the day of her launching at Union City, in 1868, and later life, when she was owned and commanded by Captain William T. Leale. Her last assignment was on the San Francisco–San Quentin run, and in this service a fair percentage of her north-bound passengers were handcuffed, heavily-guarded felons, en route from the various criminal courts to the grim walls of the state penitentiary. Captain Leale was a kindly man, and to him many a convict was indebted for his chance at rehabilitation. As practical as he was kind, Captain Leale realized that a man just out of "the big house" is up against a tough proposition in the matter of finding work, and was always ready to help out when he could. Consequently, the *Caroline* generally had a goodly

---

the customhouse, and so there always was the chance that the date of surrender would get into the record as that of the actual destruction of the vessel. This may be why the government records miss, by several weeks, the date of the big steamboat fire at Broderick in 1932.

sprinkling of ex-convicts in her crew. At last Captain Leale retired, and the weary old *Caroline* was laid up at Sausalito, where
fire of unknown origin ended her days, on November 18, 1917.

The only death recorded in later-day steamboat fires marred
the passing of the famous old *Gold,* which burned on November
8, 1920. The fire, probably from the same cause as that which
ended the days of the *Petaluma,* broke out at about one o'clock in
the morning, as the *Gold*—also fully loaded—lay at the wharf in
Petaluma. They were less fortunate with her, however; so quickly
did the flames spread that the chief engineer and a mess-boy were
obliged to leap into the creek and the mess-boy was drowned.
There was a strong wind that night, and it held the *Gold* so firmly
against the wharf that in spite of all of their efforts they were
unable to get her out into the stream. As a result, the wharf and
warehouse went, too.

The *Oriole* must have burned shortly afterward, but as she was
out of documentation by then, there is no record other than the
memory of rivermen—"The *Oriole?* Yes, she burnt up; must
have been along around the early part of '21."

At the time of the *Gold* disaster, the nation had hopefully em-
barked upon what, for one reason or another, was known as the
"Noble Experiment," a socio-legal phenomenon which is mentioned here solely because it was a contributing factor in the loss
of more than one steamboat. It marked an era, you may recall, in
which those in the upper brackets of society obtained their more
robust liquid refreshment from gentlemen who drove flashy auto-
mobiles, talked out of the corners of their mouths, and were known
on various occasions to be adept in the handling of sub-machine
guns. Those lower in the social scale, not having the required price,
got their liquor the hard way, frequently by methods which
were not entirely lacking in ingenuity. It is in this latter stratum
of society that one found those who came to be known as the
"canned-heat bums," also the "jakes," who sought escape from the
realities of life by drinking Jamaica ginger. The "canned-heat
bum" was a bedraggled, jittery sot who had learned that if he took
the contents of a popular brand of solidified fuel and squeezed it

through a rag—preferably a dirty one—he could press out a fairish quantity of denatured alcohol. Both during this process and in the ensuing state of befuddlement in which he might drop a lighted pipe or cigarette into his filthy pallet, fire was an ever-present hazard. In the jungles along the riverbanks you could always find a fair share of these social derelicts, and keeping them off any steamboats which chanced to be tied up near by was something of a problem. There are indications that several of these sorry outcasts had sought winter refuge in the cabins of either the *Alviso* or the *Weitchpec,* which were laid up at Bryte's Bend, just above Sacramento, on the night of December 15, 1920. At any rate, the fire which broke out made quick work of both of these one-time favorites of the upper river.

There were, of course, fires which had more happy endings. Such was the case of the *Dauntless,* which in some manner got alight in Stockton Slough, along about 1910. To save neighboring wharves and sheds they let her go out into midstream, filled her with water, and she settled to the bottom some eight feet below. At length she was raised in a novel manner: Two barges were towed out and made fast, one on each side of her, and heavy timbers were bridged across between them; at low water she was secured to these beams, and, as the tide rose,[4] so did the barges and the *Dauntless.* Then they moved the barges and their soggy burden into shallower water, to ground again. The next tide raised her a few feet more. Finally they got her onto the beach and pumped her out. The damage was repaired and she went on about her business, later to become the Diesel-powered freighter, *San Joaquin.*

With the dwindling of the river trade, other stern-wheelers went in other ways. Many were broken up, converted into barges, sold as shore-side resorts, or merely run onto the mud and left to rot away. The ends of three of them, while not involving fire, are not without passing interest—the case of the *J. D. Peters,* last stern-

---

[4] You get four feet of tide up at Stockton. As a matter of fact, there is a slight tide experienced even at Sacramento, during low-water periods, despite its 30-foot elevation above sea level.

San Diego Historical Society Photo

The tidal drydock at Port Isabel, with *Colorado* (No. 2) undergoing repairs

San Diego Union Photo

The pride of the Colorado was the two-stacker *Mohave* (No. 2) shown here with a
Sunday School picnic aboard at Yuma, Arizona, 1876.

Thousands have traveled in the palatial *Delta King* between San Francisco and Sacramento.

A night voyager, *Petaluma* (No. 3) works cargo during the hours
of darkness at the city for which she is named.

wheeler regularly on the Stockton run; the *Reform;* and the old S.P. "floating palace," *Navajo.* They wound up in a reclamation project, which won back for agriculture many hundreds of acres of rich farm land at Mandeville Island, following a bad break in the levee in 1938.

Holland is not alone with her problem of the dikes; it is one which more than once has brought sorrow to the fertile Delta country of the lower San Joaquin. The Bouldin Island break, for instance, was a tough one to handle; 90-foot piling, driven into the gap as a starter, merely disappeared from view in the soft peat bottom. They filled an old sailing vessel with sand and sank her in the opening—and the mud swallowed her, too. Finally, they had to go quite a distance back into the island, to where the soil was strong enough to take piling, and there build a dam to stop the flooding waters. At Mandeville the big job was not so much building the dam as it was getting rid of the water once the break was closed. To handle this end of it they took the three venerable river steamers, ran them in through the gap, and moored them with their wheels close to a planked sluiceway through the levee, scarcely above the river's level. Then they started up their engines, and the trio of old-timers, paddling away at a lively clip but getting nowhere, actually pushed the water out of the sunken island and back into the stream. Pumps finished the job, leaving the three steamboats high and dry, and they ended their days as bunkhouses for ranch hands.

And so came at last the fateful night of August 28, 1932. It was in a period of economic depression, and where there normally should have been work for many river boats, now a whole fleet of steamers and barges lay idle at Broderick, just across the river from Sacramento; the spectacle of cold steamboats, lying forlorn and alone for want of cargoes, was no unusual one in those days. Late in the evening someone living aboard a houseboat near by heard the windows rattle. Was it only a gust of wind? Had the "canned-heat bums" got aboard one of the steamers and started a row? The latter guess probably was right, although it never will be known; at any rate, the man in the houseboat got up to investigate. He hadn't far to look for the sound which had aroused him—fire and smoke were pouring from the windows of one of the fleet of steam-boats. He gave the alarm, but already it was too late.

Now the wind was increasing in force. Sheets of flame and swirling sparks rolled around the other vessels, and with amazing rapidity the conflagration spread. The alarm was answered by Sacramento's firemen, but they stopped at the river. Not only is Broderick outside the Sacramento city limits but, to make a bad matter legally worse, it is outside of Sacramento County. Suppose there had been a serious fire in Sacramento at that time, or men or apparatus had been lost while gallivanting around across the river in Yolo County? The fire chief would have had no valid excuse. And, looking at it from the practical standpoint of fire engineering, the riverbank at Broderick is not sufficiently steep-to for a pumper to draw from the stream. So about all that they would do was to watch, and to see that falling firebrands did not give Sacramento a bad waterfront fire of its own.

The little *Flora,* which many saw as the *Dixie* in *Huckleberry Finn,* burned through her lines and the south wind caught her. Against the current of the river it carried her, a floating pillar of fire, up against the I Street bridge—where her oil tanks blew up. Here was something which Sacramento's firemen could reach, and they did so with a vim. They saved the bridge, but there wasn't much that anyone could have done for the *Flora.*

"The boats are all on fire!" Second only to the rapidity with which the flames raced through the doomed fleet was the speed with which the word got around the city, and there was a general movement toward the river. Broderick's modest population was out en masse, and they were joined by those who ran or drove across the two bridges from Sacramento. It seems that there was a big dance in town that night, and the spectacle of dowagers and debu-tantes, lifting long dresses and trying to keep expensive slippers from being ruined in the deep summer dust of Broderick's water front, added a distinct society-page flavor to the affair. It also added no little to the difficulties of those who were trying to do something more useful than merely look at a fire.

A government tug joined the *Flora* in her death agony. Men in other tugs and launches braved the tornado of fire and smoke to get lines onto the *Dover* and the *Red Bluff,* which at last were towed to safety. An ugly pall of smoke drifted away, lighted by flames which made it visible for miles.

"There it goes—watch it!" A tall smokestack would totter as its guys or their supporting timbers burned away, and then plunge down sidewise into the flames. Little whirlwinds of smoke and hot gas danced away, across the water and over the trees lining the shore. A sudden puff, an increase in the intensity of the fire—and they knew that an oil tank had let go; a mounting pillar of sparks would come as a pilothouse or texas, its underpinning destroyed, tumbled into the tornado of fire with a crash which was scarcely louder than the roaring of the flames themselves.

And then, little by little, the fire died down—died because there was nothing left to feed it. In the morning, sodden hulks and heaps of glowing embers around the tangled ironwork of engines or hog-frames alone remained of the little fleet of river steamers. Besides the *Flora,* the *Colusa* was gone. So were the *San Jose,* the *Valletta,* the *San Joaquin No. 2* and the *San Joaquin No. 4*—the latter once touted as "the most powerful inland vessel in America." The one-time pride of the Farmers' Transportation Company, the *Sacramento,* never would haul cargo again. Neither would an assortment of barges and small craft whose timbers had been so consumed as to expose, still smoking hot, the long driftbolts which once had given them strength. And that other inanimate but none the less important player in *Huckleberry Finn*—the *Jacinto*—had passed with the *Flora* beyond the fiery gates through which there is no return.

CHAPTER XV

THE RIVER GROWS DARK

𝕴T WAS UP AROUND Collinsville, and already the pilothouse
windows were rattling to the strong wind, although it was late
spring, and the night was as clear as a bell. Ahead, low on the
water, lay a dozen or more bobbing lights.

"Fishermen," said the pilot. "See 'em?

"Those are lanterns on the nets," he went on. "They're sup-
posed to make one end of the net fast on shore and buoy the other
end with a float or a skiff, with a light on it. Generally they keep
clear, but not always. Sometimes they string right out into the
fairway and expect you to go around—if you can. And it isn't
too good an idea to run through 'em, either, especially in these
Diesel jobs. They get in your propeller—worse than with a stern-
wheeler. There you'd just wrap a few turns around the wheel and
go paddling along without much damage to yourself; the nets
would tear themselves up in a little while.

"Sometimes, when you get close, one of 'em will start yelling
'Ah, Meester—Save-a-da-net! Save-a-da-net!'—and then, if you
don't give him what he thinks he's entitled to in the way of room,
he'll add some smart crack like 'You sonna-ma-beetch!' In the

old days, sometimes they'd take a pot shot at you as you went by. Then the boys took to carrying shotguns in the pilothouses. You know how it is—now and then you'll get a good shot at a flock of ducks, or something. Funny thing; about that time, the fishermen quit shooting at us.

"Look—there's the *Yuba,* coming down. First one we've met tonight. I can remember times when we'd have met up with a dozen boats by now; there'd be hay schooners[1] and steamboats all along the run to Sacramento, or potato boats in among the islands on the way to Stockton. Will we see any more tonight? Oh, maybe a little tanker, or a tug with a sand barge in tow, but nothing else."

The fishermen were astern now, and so was the *Yuba*—Diesel-powered, like ourselves. Overhead, the stars burned intensely bright. The banks and all the country behind them were inky-black, and the river itself was a murky ribbon, scarcely less gloomy than the shores which so dimly defined it. The pilothouse was dark and silent, the mullions of the small-paned windows a mere black grid against the slightly less intense darkness outside; there was no illumination but the watchman's cigarette, and a diffused red glow from the binnacle-light.[2] Conversation lagged; thoughts were on happier days of river boating—or happier nights, when instead of a sleeping crew the vessel might have carried, down below, a group of happy if not too melodious singers in what once had been a well-stocked bar.

On the road atop the levee close by, a truck sped past. A truck —yes, that was what had done it; trucks, good roads, and a desire,

[1] Although she was a flat-bottomed scow and square at each end, the Sacramento River schooner, now extinct, was far from being an ugly duckling. Her centerboard enabled her to work to windward rather nicely, in spite of a deckload of baled hay so high that it was necessary to double-reef in order to get the booms up off of the bales and she had to be steered from a jury wheel carried on a pulpit rigged atop the deckload. Light, and with started sheets, anything like a decent breeze would give her an amazing turn of speed.

[2] Rather recently scientific research has led to the important discovery that the human eye more readily accustoms itself for night-vision after being exposed to red rays than to those of any other color—a discovery which was acclaimed with no small amount of praise. When they heard of it, rivermen merely chuckled. They had been using red binnacle-lamps, and red lights for reading charts, for a generation, having discovered the same thing without the aid of laboratory research.

above everything else in the world, for more speed and more profits. Since 1926, and even before, the star of the river steamboats had been dimming, even as the river itself was growing dark in the absence of the glistening steamers which passed in the night.

It was in 1926 that steam navigation on California's rivers reached what may be called its peak, for that was the year in which the magnificent *Delta King* and *Delta Queen* were built. With steel hulls prefabricated on the Clyde, they were set up in the yards at Stockton, and were the last word in luxurious inland liners—1,837 gross tons, 250 feet long, each with a pair of boilers which carried 225 pounds pressure and 2,000-horsepower compound engines with a stroke of 10 feet. There were ample promenade decks, and huge curved hoods over the big stern wheels protected those in the after part of the vessel from spray or noise. Inside was a spacious dining room with plate-glass windows and a profusion of hardwood trim; a stained-glass dome gave a touch of color to the comfortable social hall. The staterooms left nothing to be desired, and a traditionally fine cuisine had been handed down from the days of the *Chrysopolis* and the *New World*. The two *Deltas* —which left San Francisco at 6:30 P.M. on alternate days—were favorites for years.

Simultaneously with the delivery of these two fine steamers came the opening of the Antioch Toll Bridge—and highway competition which they could not hope to stem. But they kept on bravely in the face of dwindling revenues, even though, in the winter months, they frequently made the trip with only a corporal's guard of passengers; the river steamboat was through. In the winter of 1932 the Stockton passenger trade folded up, with the *J. D. Peters*—later to dig herself a quiet grave in Mandeville Island —making the last run to that city on Christmas Day. At about the same time it was announced that the big boats on the Sacramento no longer would stop at Rio Vista. True, they still got heavy summer patronage in passengers, and a good share of freight; but the winter travel was gone.

In November 1941 the *Delta King* and the *Delta Queen* were withdrawn from the Sacramento and were laid up, thus ending some ninety-three years of passenger service on the California rivers. A buyer appeared from the Hudson, and plans were made to board up the windows of the two *Deltas* and send them around to the East Coast; it would have been, perhaps, a fitting reversal of the process of nearly a century before, when the Hudson had contributed tonnage to the Sacramento and the San Joaquin. And then—Pearl Harbor. The two big vessels were taken over by the government, for use around San Francisco Bay, and their gleaming white vanished under somber wartime paint, as they became the *U.S.S. Delta King* and the *U.S.S. Delta Queen*. The *Isleton*, re-engined with Diesels, joined the Army under the odd name of the *Army Queen*. The *Port of Stockton*, ex-*Capital City*, joined up too, as did the rebuilt *H. J. Corcoran*, known in her later years as the *Crockett*, and the *Fort Sutter*.

And so it remains for one of the little creek steamboats to keep alive, for a time at least, the story of steam navigation on the streams of California—the creek steamboats which, since the first paddle wheels turned in the Golden State nearly a century ago, have played a far from unimportant part in the inland navigation of the West. Away back in 1850—the exact date was December 2—the first *Sacramento* steamed up Alviso Creek, at the south end of San Francisco Bay, with passengers for San Jose. Rightly speaking, Alviso Creek is a tidal estuary, and the *United States Coast Pilot* speaks of it merely as Alviso Slough. But in its palmy days, when San Jose was the state capital, it was important enough, and many a California politico of that period made his way to the source of laws and jobs by steamboat to Alviso, and then on by ox team to San Jose. Then Colonel Peter Donahue built the railroad—now a part of the Southern Pacific main line—to San Jose from San Francisco, and put an end to the need for steamboats on that run. The Alviso boats, incidentally, made Union City as an intermediate stop, reaching it by Alameda Creek. You won't find Union City on the charts any more, for its name long ago was changed to Alvarado—and Alameda Creek, which enters the Bay a few miles north of the Dumbarton Toll Bridge, isn't even mentioned in the *Sailing Directions*.

Colonel Donahue's name is one to remember in California history. His ironworks built steamboat engines, and he himself built railroads. His memory is kept green by the Mechanics' Fountain on lower Market Street in San Francisco—a beautiful thing, whose sculptor, Douglas Tilden, lived in those happy days before it was considered necessary for all statues to have Slavic features, size-18 necks, dropsical ankles, and puffy hands with fingers like bloated bananas. The fountain was presented by his son, for whom was named that swift little side-wheeler on the Petaluma run, the *James M. Donahue.*

There were, too, the steamboats of the Napa River, which roughly parallels Petaluma Creek and comes down between Vallejo and Mare Island to empty into Carquinez Strait. It was in 1850 that the *Dolphin* was put on the Napa run, to ply back and forth in company with the *Anna Abernethy,* the *Sophie,* the *Paul Pry,* and the *Commodore Jones,* the latter named for Commodore Thomas ap Catesby Jones, U.S.N., commander of the Pacific Squadron. Later the *Guadalupe* took passengers to Napa and Suscol, with connections for White Sulphur Springs, and toward the end of her days, even the famous *New World* was listed as available for travelers to Napa. Considering the size of the *New World,* however, it is probable that this advertisement was a bit of poetic license in the steamboat schedules; it is more likely that her passengers got there by transfer to a smaller vessel, just as the *Cleopatra* operated as a feeder-boat for the larger *Amelia.*

Charles Minturn, in addition to his connection with other steamboat enterprises in California, was a pioneer in Petaluma Creek operations, starting service from San Francisco to Lakeview, on the creek a few miles below Petaluma, in 1860; from that point, passengers went on to San Rafael, Bodega, Santa Rosa, Healdsburg, and Ukiah by stagecoach. Two years later he improved the channel by dredging, and opened a 2½-mile railroad line, with horse-drawn cars, from Haystack Landing into Petaluma itself. Later the creek was dredged all the way to its head. It is really a narrow estuary, and its water is salt. But so tortuous is its course and so strong are its currents at certain stages of the tide that its navigation is a job for a competent river pilot. Minturn was its pioneer, although its navigation had been tried, three years before, by the little side-wheeler, *Rambler*. A contemporary woodcut, however, reveals the *Rambler* in what probably was a characteristic pose—her passengers are all out on her forward deck with poles, trying to push her off of a mud flat among the tules. It may be only a winding slough, but Petaluma Creek is a fitting place for discussion as we near the end of the story of the California steamboats. Down on the Embarcadero let us try not to look at the now meaningless gold-leaf letters on the windows of The River Lines' offices on Pier 3—"Fast Steamers to Sacramento."

Alongside Pier 3 lies a little stern-wheeler, the last of the commercial steamboats in the state. She has a box-like superstructure, and an odd-looking elevator capable of accommodating a sizable lift truck is located just forward of her pilothouse. Unlike other inland steamers, her small, thin stack is located far aft,[3] like that of the single-end coastwise steam schooners of the early days. She could do with a bit of paint; but everyone is too busy for such things these days; besides, she probably can do her work just as well without it. She is the Petaluma and Santa Rosa Railroad's steamer *Petaluma,* third to bear the name.

At about 5:30 in the afternoon the last of her cargo is aboard— an assortment of plunder and poultry feed consigned to the merchants of Petaluma or, by transshipment on trains of the Northwestern Pacific, to Santa Rosa or Sebastopol or Healdsburg, or perhaps even as far as Eureka. Her lines are let go; a resonant "Bong! Bong!" comes from her engine-room gong—she is innocent of such modern refinements as the engine telegraph—and her big wheel begins to turn. A prolonged, quavering blast comes from her whistle, and she backs out into the Bay.

Is the little steamer merely whistling in accordance with the *U.S. Pilot Rules?* Or is she whistling to keep up her courage as

---

[3] This innovation, intended to keep perishable cargo from being stowed between the engines and the boiler-room, was viewed with no little alarm by the engine-room unions, who saw in it a move to have the engineer act as fireman as well.

she goes on, alone, in the gathering darkness? The Captains Four-att are gone from the rivers—grandfather, father, and sons. So are Captain John Leale and his scarcely less famous brother—and Van Pelt, Chadwick, Baxter, and the rest. The *Petaluma* won't meet the slim *Antelope* coming down from Donahue's Landing tonight, nor the *Gold,* nor the *Clinton.* They're gone, now, all gone—but can we be sure she won't meet their ghosts, especially if it comes on a bit foggy? We can hardly blame the little *Petaluma* for the slight quaver in the note of her whistle.

Bravely, albeit slowly, she plods along past Angel Island, and up beyond Red Rock and The Brothers and into San Pablo Bay, where she swings off to port as the pilot lays his course through the narrow dredged channel across that shallow sheet of water, toward Black Point, at the mouth of Petaluma Creek. One by one the channel marks are checked off in the logbook, for even on the clearest night she is navigated by the compass course steered and the number of minutes and seconds on each heading. The pilot admits that this may look a bit odd, but maintains that it would be bad practice to do it any other way.

"Suppose it's foggy tomorrow night?" he says. There is the answer: he must keep an accurate record of each night's work, so that if on the following night nothing is visible but a wall of gray, he will know how to reach his destination.

Now the red lights on the drawbridges across the entrance to the creek are close at hand, and again the *Petaluma* sounds a long blast. There is an answering signal from ashore, and the string of lights begins to move; the span is opening. Now the lights turn to green—the channel is clear, and the little steamboat paddles through. The bridges swing shut behind her, and she heads on, up the winding slough.

From the creek's mouth to the head of navigation she will alter her course approximately fifty times, and the pilot will be a busy man; he must remember all of those courses, by points and quarter-points, and how long he has to remain on each heading. Over the steering-compass is mounted a watch with an over-size second-hand, and with the aid of these two the pilot goes on. Some courses will be as long as seven minutes; the shortest one is thirty seconds. Twin House, The Haystacks, Cloudy Bend—he checks them off in his log, and the *Petaluma* plods on, through a channel so narrow that at times you can all but touch each bank with an oar. Motionless and silent in the night, cows peer at the maritime intruder in the midst of their pastures.

Now the lights of Petaluma loom up ahead, and the crew, most of whom have been sleeping below, begin to appear. The steamer deftly executes a 90-degree turn in the tiny basin at the head of the creek, and swings in alongside the pier. If the tide is out,[4] there will be lots of work for the elevator in the forward part of the vessel as she unloads. The pilot yawns, and guesses that he'll catch a few winks while they are tied up; the crew, now fully aroused, are busying themselves with the job of trundling cargo out on the wharf or directly into waiting railway cars. It is about midnight, the run of some thirty-six miles up from San Francisco taking anywhere from six to eight hours, depending upon the stage of the tide.

With startling rapidity, the *Petaluma* is cleared of her cargo. And now the job of loading begins. Eggs—eggs—more eggs. It is an agricultural community, and the chicken farms of Petaluma are famous for their output; not for nothing is the city known as "The Egg-Basket of the West."

The Petaluma & Santa Rosa Railroad is connected with the Northwestern Pacific—and the Northwestern Pacific is a part of Southern Pacific's family. This, in a way, makes the *Petaluma* an S.P. steamer, and with no small pride her people claim that she is the fastest division of the huge system, in the point of cargo-handling. Truly, the *Petaluma* is a marvel of speed. Up goes the elevator—out goes the lift truck to a waiting car—on goes another truck—and down goes the elevator. Roaring steam from the engine which runs the lift is heard above the rumble of trucks and the infrequent voices of those who handle the cargo. Meanwhile, Petaluma sleeps, secure in the knowledge that there will be grain

---

[4] At the spring stages, the tide at Petaluma has a range of 13 feet—greater than that of any other California city.

on hand for feeding the poultry and that today's eggs will promptly reach the markets of San Francisco and beyond.

And now there comes a hush; the last of the San Francisco–bound cargo is on board, and the pilot is climbing up the ladder at the after end of the texas, to take over again; already the wheel is revolving slowly, as the engineer warms up his machinery. The *Petaluma* backs down against a spring-line, to swing her bow out into the turning basin, which is not much larger than herself. It's a neat bit of seamanship, and one which the pilot has been practicing successfully for a long time. The spring-line drops into the water as she gets into position to make the opening from the basin into the creek. It is about three o'clock in the morning, and the *Petaluma* is on her own again. Once more the voice of her whistle is raised, and the banks of the creek again echo back the "Chung, chung, chung, chung! Chung, chung, chung, chung!" of her paddles. Sleepy freight clerks give her a farewell glance as she heads away from town, down the creek. One by one, lights on the loading platform go out, and the *Petaluma* vanishes around the first bend.

The last steamboat on a California stream is going home.

CHAPTER XVI

AND THEN THERE WERE THE FERRIES

*I*MPORTANT as was the part which California's river steamers played, it would be a mistake to assume that they were the only participants in the state's inland navigation. The total number of travelers by steamboat to the up-river communities would be insignificant beside the astronomical figure representing the ferry traffic on San Francisco Bay alone.

It is, of course, San Francisco Bay which first comes to mind when one mentions ferry boats in California. In the heyday of the ferries, vessels of the Southern Pacific system alone carried 40,211,535 people in a single year; that was in 1930. Add to that the millions who crossed the Bay each year by Key Route, Northwestern Pacific, and Richmond and San Rafael—to say nothing of the passengers between San Francisco and Vallejo in the Monticello Steamship Company steamers—and you will get an idea of how big it was.

And San Francisco was not alone. Disregarding entirely the

chain ferries of the rivers, the San Pedro–Terminal Island ferry *Islander,* and the gas boats on the harbors of Los Angeles and San Diego, there were paddle-wheel vessels which plied for years on the waters of Humboldt and San Diego bays; in fact, the stern-wheeler *Antelope* still carries passengers between Eureka and the big mills across Humboldt Bay; she was built in 1910, and has the engines from a former craft of the same name, built in 1888. Ferry service between Eureka and Arcata began, so the story goes, with a little stern-wheeler called the *Glide*—of which, unfortunately, little is known—away back in 1854; later it involved the stern-wheelers *Ada, Annie, Alta, Oneatta, Phoenix, Poco Tiempo,* and, for a time, the well-known Sacramento River steamer *Weitchpec.*

Far to the south, the little flat-bottomed side-wheeler *Benicia,* built in 1881, was a San Diego pioneer. The only walking-beam ferry on San Diego Bay, she made her last crossing to Coronado on July 4, 1903. The side-wheeler *Coronado* came out in 1886; and in 1888 what probably was the first propeller-driven ferry in the West, the big *Silver Gate*—a $400,000 headache for her owners —was launched at Coronado. It has been said of the *Silver Gate*'s designer that his mother must have been frightened by the Crystal Palace; at any rate, she was a maritime example of the gingerbread architecture of the era. Notable largely for her unwieldiness and her inability to stop at the end of a run, she had but a short career, becoming, in turn, a floating dance-hall and the quarters for the San Diego Yacht Club. Dry-rot caught up with her aged hulk in 1920. San Diego's other paddle-wheel vessels were the *Ramona,* built in 1903, and the *Morena,* which came out in 1920 and ran for some twenty years; she was the last inland steam vessel on San Diego Bay. All were owned by the San Diego & Coronado Ferry Company.

To return to San Francisco: In 1826, John Reed built a sloop to carry travelers across the Bay to what now is Sausalito; the first ferry passengers crossed to the Contra Costa shores in two little schooners which Captain William Richardson made available in 1835, and while the tariffs have not been preserved they no doubt were attractive—at least, to the captain. In those days, impatient people could get across in a wherry for $50 a head, and one may assume that Richardson did not operate at a loss. Inflation is nothing new.

In 1850 the little steamer *Kangaroo* was placed in regular service between San Francisco and the hamlets across the Bay, and she was followed the next year by another (former Stockton) river steamboat, the *Erastus Corning.* Operator of the latter was Charles Minturn, doing business under the firm name of Contra Costa Steam Navigation Company. Other packets on the East Bay ferry running at about the same time were the *Boston,* the *Red Jacket,* and the *General Sutter,* of which the first two were well known in the river trade.

As one might expect, competition was not long in developing. James B. Larue, who organized the Oakland and San Antonio Steam Navigation Company, set out to get all of the business which he could develop or take away from Minturn—or, for that matter, from any of the half-dozen independents who also had got into the game. Soon the *Caleb Cope,* the *Hector,* and the *Jenny Lind* deserted river and creek for this lush new field, and the rosy days of the one-dollar fare were over. Larue chopped it to half a dollar, Minturn to a quarter; an independent owner named Wingate came in with a boat which took passengers at a dime a head. The rate-war was short, Minturn and Larue finally agreeing to stabilize the price at twenty-five cents. In 1858 Larue cut this in half and there was another big row, but he soon went back to the old rate.

Minturn had, meanwhile, entered the northern ferry trade, running steamers from San Francisco to San Quentin and Lakeville, where they connected with stages. This was in 1860, and one of his boats was the original *Contra Costa*—not to be confused with the later car-ferry of the same name—which was an important figure both on this run and in the East Bay service, as will be seen later.

The direct ancestor of the Southern Pacific fleet was, in fact, the *Contra Costa;* she was a little single-ender, and she entered the East Bay field on September 1, 1863, under the banner of the San Francisco and Oakland Railroad Company. She ran from Gibbons' Point, about where Oakland Pier now is located, to a landing between the Broadway and Vallejo Street wharves in San Francisco, and made six round trips a day. Minturn was, of course, her owner.

One is inclined to think that the term Damon and Pythias never could be applied to Larue and Minturn; for at about the time the *Contra Costa* started on the Oakland run the two transportation tycoons were at it again, hammer and tongs. This time it was a lawsuit which had to do with Larue's alleged violation of the ferry monopoly which Minturn had wangled from the town trustees of Oakland. By the time the thing got to the Supreme Court the two had made up, and they ran their fleets jointly until 1865, when Larue sold his boats to the railroad. The next year Minturn withdrew, and thereafter confined himself largely to Marin and Sonoma County transportation.

What might be termed the modern era of Alameda service began on August 25, 1864, when the San Francisco & Alameda Railroad Company put the *Sophie McLean* on the run between the Davis Street Wharf in San Francisco and a landing near the foot of Pacific Avenue in Alameda. Later they added the original *Alameda* to this run, and she had the distinction of meeting the first transcontinental train, which came in to Alameda over the Central Pacific on September 6, 1869. Two months later, use of the temporary terminal at Alameda ended, and trains began using the newly constructed Oakland Wharf. Control of the two little East Bay railroads by this time had passed into the hands of the "Big Four"—Stanford, Hopkins, Crocker, and Huntington—who founded the present Southern Pacific.

San Antonio Creek, better known as Oakland Creek or as Oakland Estuary, was an artery of ferry traffic for many years. Originally unusable because of a sand bar at its mouth, it was dredged in 1859. Regular ferry service on the "Creek Route" did not start, however, until July 1, 1876, when the famous river steamer *Capital* was put on this run. In later years a vehicular route almost exclusively, it saw its trade grow steadily as the *Encinal* and the *Melrose,* former Alameda boats, were joined by the second *Thorough-*

Southern Pacific's *Piedmont* and Key Route's *San Jose*
on San Francisco Bay about 1904

The single-ender *James M. Donahue* was a commuters' favorite on
the Marin County run for many years.

H. R. Fitch Photo

(*Above*) One of the world's first propeller-driven ferries, the *Silver Gate* had a brief career at San Diego, in 1888.

(*Left*) Still running on San Francisco Bay, the *Berkeley* retains her Gay 'Nineties motif, stained-glass windows and all.

fare, a 2,605-ton giant. It was a long trip—about forty-five minutes—from the Ferry Building to the landing at the foot of Broadway in Oakland, but it had its compensation. For one thing, you
had plenty of time to see what the chef was up to, in the tidy dining room on the texas deck. There are those who argue that the
food on the Creek boats was no better than that on, for instance,
the *Oakland* or the *Fernwood,* but that is a moot point. At any
rate, you had more time to enjoy it. The Creek boats ran until
1926, when the Oakland Pier was opened up to automobile traffic.

Car-transfer ferries were in use on San Francisco Bay for many
years, the first being the original *Thoroughfare,* which ran from
1871 until 1909; later her discarded hulk was filled with rock and
sunk as a foundation for the Dumbarton Bridge. Two passenger
ferries, the *Newark* and the *Bay City,* also doubled as car-transfers,
having tracks on their lower decks to accommodate the cars of the
old narrow-gauge line in Alameda. In 1879 the *Garden City* was
added to the Alameda run, as was the *Encinal* in 1888. By this
time Southern Pacific had taken over the narrow-gauge line, which
James G. Fair and his associates had planned for the eastern shore
of the Bay. To old-time San Franciscans, so long as the ferries ran,
boats to Alameda were called "The Narrow Gauge," whereas, if
you were planning to go to Oakland you said that you were going
over on "The Broad Gauge."

The Ferry Building, by many considered San Francisco's outstanding landmark, was completed in 1898, and the ferries which
had been using a landing just to the north of the present location
shifted their operations to the new terminal. A marvel of efficiency,
this building each day handled teeming thousands of commuters
with speed and relative comfort; it was definitely a part of old
San Francisco.

Time was marching on. One by one, the single-end boats
passed out of service, to be replaced by the conventional double-end
ferry, which does not have to be backed out of its slip and turned
around. Oil fuel was taking the place of coal; and some thought
was being devoted to the possibility of using propellers instead of
the more cumbersome side wheels—although such side-wheelers

continued to be built for several years, and the *Oakland,* the *Piedmont,* the *Garden City,* and the *Newark* were long-time favorites. In 1898 the steel-hulled *Berkeley,* one of the first successful propeller-driven double-enders on the coast, was launched; others soon followed. The Key Route's fine fleet of orange-colored steamers, beginning with the original 1,115-ton *Yerba Buena* and the *San Jose* in 1903, all were propeller-driven.

Next of the Key ferries were the 621-ton *San Francisco* in 1905, and the slightly larger *Fernwood* and *Claremont* two years later. They were wooden, with high-pressure, triple-expansion engines, and were strictly passenger vessels, no freight or vehicles being carried. The Key System—or San Francisco, Oakland & San Jose Railway Company, as it originally was called—ran from the Ferry Building to a long, open-deck trestle which accommodated electric trains for Oakland, Claremont, and Berkeley, as well as the interurbans of the Oakland, Antioch & Eastern Railway. The trestle came out from the vicinity of Emeryville almost to Goat Island, and paralleled the present easterly span of the Bay Bridge; the tracks, in fact, dipped down into the same underpass which today conducts the bridge trains under the main-line railway tracks. The style of trains through the tunnel has changed; but the odor has not.

The Key people stuck to propeller-driven vessels, with the lone exception of the *Treasure Island,* which they acquired in later years for hauling visitors to the Golden Gate International Exposition in 1939. She had been the *San Pedro,* of 1,720 tons, built in 1911 for the Atchison, Topeka & Santa Fe Railway; they had used her and the *San Pablo,* which came out in 1900, for connecting with their trains at Point Richmond. Both were side-wheelers. Later Key System ferries included the turbine-electric *Hayward,* the *San Leandro,* the *Peralta,* and the second *Yerba Buena.* The last two were steel vessels of 2,075 gross tons, built in 1927, and were the last steam ferries constructed in California. Following an unfortunate accident, the *Peralta* was sold; rebuilt and re-engined with Diesels, she took up a new life on Puget Sound as the streamliner *Kalakala.*

A favorite for many years, and on many runs, was the old *El Capi-*

tan, built in 1868; her walking-beam engine came from an Eastern lake steamer which had burned. This engine, built in 1845, ran her back and forth across the Bay until about 1916, when she was transferred to the Vallejo Junction run; there, for the first time in nearly half a century, she had a day off each week. She was on the active list until 1921, when she was laid up, and four years later she went to the wreckers. One wonders how much of today's machinery is being built to last for seventy-six years.

Steam ferry service to Sausalito, on anything other than a hit-or-miss basis, began on May 10, 1868, when the Sausalito Land & Ferry Company put the single-end side-wheeler *Princess* on the run. Next came the propeller-driven *Diana*—a former yacht— and in 1874 the land company bought the side-wheeler *Petaluma* from Minturn, renamed her *Petaluma of Sausalito,* and added her to their fleet. Before long this double-jointed name appears to have palled a bit upon everyone, and she became the first *Tamalpais.* Meanwhile the San Rafael & San Quentin Railroad bought the *Clinton* and the *Contra Costa* from Minturn and put them on the San Rafael run. The following year Peter Donahue's railroad, the San Francisco & North Pacific, opened its rail service from Santa Rosa to Donahue Landing, south of Petaluma, connecting with boats for San Francisco. The original San Francisco landing for the Marin-Sonoma boats was Meiggs' Wharf; later it was moved to Davis Street, and eventually to the Ferry Building.

Rail lines to serve communities in Marin and Sonoma counties continued to expand, and their connecting ferry services grew. In 1903 the North Shore Railroad Company changed over to stand-ard-gauge from the narrow-gauge which was the mode for that area, electrified its lines, and also built the big double-ender *Cazadero.* The Northwestern Pacific Railroad Company, the name best known to Marin commuters, was formed in 1907, tak-ing in all of the little railroad lines in the area. Owned jointly by the Southern Pacific and the Santa Fe, this line passed to the sole ownership of the former in 1928. Its fleet, as the little single-enders went out of business, included those old stand-bys of the north-shore commuters, the *Ukiah,* the *Tiburon,* the second *Tamal-*

pais, and the second *Sausalito*. In addition to the daily commuter trade, these ferries handled thousands of tourists and picnickers to Muir Woods and Mount Tamalpais, over the famous "Crooked-est Railroad in the World," whose Double Bow-Knot Curve was known to rail fans far and wide.

The husky vessels of the Golden Gate Ferries got into the game, primarily as vehicle boats, in the Fabulous 'Twenties. They were propeller vessels, with Diesel-electric drive, and in keeping with the company's name they bore such designations as *Golden Bear, Golden Gate,* and *Golden West*. They ran from a slip at the foot of Hyde Street in San Francisco, and later were merged with Southern Pacific under the name of Southern Pacific–Golden Gate Ferries, Ltd. The same outfit ran auto ferries from Hyde Street to a long wharf in Berkeley, for several years.

Another line which went in for propeller-driven craft was the Richmond–San Rafael Ferry & Transportation Company, which has survived the bridges and still handles a large volume of traffic across the northern part of San Francisco Bay. Their *City of San Rafael* was a side-wheeler; but their others, which included the *El Paso,* the *Klamath,* the *Russian River,* and the *Sonoma Valley,* all were propeller-driven.

Perhaps not correctly ferries—although they plied regularly in the intra-Bay trade—were the fast little steamers of the Monticello Steamship Line, which maintained service from San Francisco to Vallejo and Mare Island. Of this little fleet only the *Asbury Park*— later the *City of Sacramento*—remained on the Bay until 1944, when she was sent to Puget Sound.

The big, steel-hulled *Alameda,* second of her name, was built in 1913, a 2,302-ton vessel with a length of 293 feet; she was followed a year later by the *Santa Clara,* of the same length and outward appearance but of slightly less tonnage. In 1920 the *Oakland,* ex-*Chrysopolis,* again was rebuilt, and the following year the *Newark* was withdrawn from service, to emerge, practically a new vessel, as the *Sacramento*. At about the same time Northwestern Pacific's *Ukiah* was extensively altered and became the present *Eureka.*

Western Pacific's big propeller-driven *Edward T. Jeffrey*—ex-*Feather River*—joined the Southern Pacific fleet in 1933 and was renamed *Sierra Nevada;* one of the first things they did was to hide her somber reddish-brown paint with gleaming white. She had been used for years to meet Western Pacific's trains at that company's mole, just north of Oakland Estuary, and was noted for having the deepest, most sonorous whistle of any ferry on the Bay.

And, speaking of the superlatives, the coveted title of "largest ferryboat in the world" passed from the car-transfer *Solano* to the second *Contra Costa,* when the latter was built in 1914. The new vessel registered 5,373 gross tons and was 433 feet long; she could digest four cuts of cars at one bite, and was in use until 1930, when Southern Pacific opened its bridge across Suisun Bay. Four years later she was sold, and what is left of her hulk lies at Morrow Cove, near the tollhouse of the Carquinez Bridge.

It was the building of the East Bay Bridge in 1936 which put the Oakland, Alameda, and Berkeley ferries out of the commuter trade; similarly, the contemporary Golden Gate Bridge gave the *coup de grace* to the ferries on the Marin run. All that are left are the automobile route from Richmond to San Rafael, the limited service which Southern Pacific is allowed to maintain to serve its trains at Oakland Pier, and the ferries to the shipyards. For speed we have given up the comfort of fresh air, ample seats, and the chance to save a bit of time by having breakfast—or some other meal—aboard. The friendly games of bridge or pinochle while going to and from work are a thing of the past. No longer will the tired commuter lean in relaxation over the rail on the afterdeck, his nostrils tingling with the smell of salt arising from the lathery foam that speeds astern from the huge paddle wheels, and watch the sun go down behind San Francisco's hills. And crossing the Bay in a fog has ceased to be an adventure. Of course, if you are going to meet a train, you still can go over in a ferry, and you can even get a cup of coffee and a hot dog, over a counter on the upper deck of the *Sacramento,* the *Eureka,* or the *Berkeley* — whose stained-glass windows, in the monitor roof of her upper cabin, are a last nostalgic reminder of the Gay 'Nineties. But the big dining rooms themselves are dark and empty, and the crowds are but a fraction of what they were.

What became of the rest of the fleet? They were scattered far and wide. Boarded up for sea, the *Yosemite* was sent, under her own steam, all the way down through the Panama Canal and around the shoulder of Brazil to Montevideo. The stately old *Melrose* already was gone; she had been turned into a sport-fishing barge, and was lost in a gale off the Southern California coast in 1931. War-transportation needs of the shipyards took the *Hayward,* the *San Leandro,* the *Alameda,* the *Santa Clara,* and the *City of Sacramento.* They sold the *Golden Age,* the *Golden Poppy,* and the *Golden Shore* to Puget Sound interests, who renamed them the *Klahanie,* the *Chetzmoka,* and the *Elwha;* the *Stockton* and the *Fresno* wound up in Puget Sound too, as the *Klickatat* and the *Willapa.* At San Diego, the *Golden West* emerged from a shipyard rebuilt as the *North Island.* The *Elwha,* after serving on Puget Sound, was sold to the San Diego & Coronado Ferry Company and was towed south, along the length of the Pacific Coast, to become the *Silver Strand.* And the *Encinal,* her engines removed, eventually became a night club.

Not long ago a traveler from Maine paid his first visit to San Francisco, coming in by train to Oakland Pier and crossing over in one of the last of the ferries. He got his first look at San Francisco's impressive skyline from under the span of the East Bay Bridge, with electric trains roaring overhead. Friends who had met him anxiously awaited his reaction to the pride of Western progress, which was not long in coming. For some moments he looked sourly at the bridge. Then—

"God! Why did they let them do that?"

Appendix A

STEAMBOATS OF THE CALIFORNIA RIVERS

Key to Symbols: A, abandoned; B, broken up; C, lost by collision; CR, Colorado River steamer; D, dismantled; E, lost by explosion; EC, built on East Coast; F, lost by fire; Fo, foundered; R, rebuilt; SA, sold to aliens; Sn, snagged; Str, stranded; US, sold to United States government.

The minus sign before the date indicates that the vessel is not in the record for that particular year, but has been listed in the last available publication up to that time. As the first official list of American merchant vessels is for 1868, the notation "—1868" occurs with some frequency.

Name	Type	Tons	Length	When Built	Disposal and Date
A. C. Freese	Stern-Wheeler	205	119	1886	—1917
Acme	Stern-Wheeler	294	177.5	1889	D 1911
Aetna	Stern-Wheeler	...	...	—1850	—1868
Alice	Stern-Wheeler	74.21	...	—1868	—1881
Alice Garratt	Stern-Wheeler	485	150.0	1873	—1888
Alta	Stern-Wheeler	...	...	1866	—1868
Alvarado	Stern-Wheeler	49.22	69	1870	—1890
Alviso	Stern-Wheeler	197	115	1895	F 1920
Amador	Side-Wheeler	985	221	1869	D 1905
Amelia	Side-Wheeler	385.96	147	1863	—1885
American Eagle (iron)	Side-Wheeler	...	...	EC1851	E 1853
Anna Abernethy	Side-Wheeler	...	...	—1856	—1868
Ann Arbor		...	...	—1853	—1868
Antelope	Side-Wheeler	581.05	202.6	EC1847	B 1888
Apache	Stern-Wheeler	938.89	207	1880	D 1928
Aurora	Stern-Wheeler	406	145	1885	A 1932
Banner		175.25	...	—1868	—1881
Bear (snag boat)	Stern-Wheeler	242	157.8	1921	D 1926
Belle (No. 1)	Stern-Wheeler	95.12	...	1853	E 1856
Belle (No. 2)	Stern-Wheeler	89.70	93.5	1865	Sn 1870
Benicia	Stern-Wheeler	...	...	—1850	—1868
Boston		71	...	1851	—1877
Brisk	Side-Wheeler	132.48	122	1869	—1885
Buena City		...	...	—1854	—1868
Bullion	Stern-Wheeler	147.46	116.2	1874	—1888
Butte		26	...	1850	—1868
C. M. Small	Stern-Wheeler	207.89	110.7	1872	—1895
C. M. Weber	Side-Wheeler	144	...	1851	—1868
Caleb Cope	Side-Wheeler	73	...	1851	—1868
California	Side-Wheeler	763.50	...	EC—1850	—1868
Camanche	Side-Wheeler	148	...	EC1851	—1868
Capital	Side-Wheeler	1,989.20	277	1866	B 1896

135

Name	Type	Tons	Length	When Built	Disposal and Date
Capital City[a]	Stern-Wheeler	1,142	220	1910	US 1942
Captain Sutter	Side-Wheeler	...	...	1849	—1868
Captain Weber	Stern-Wheeler	612.71	174.5	1892	F 1943
Caroline	Stern-Wheeler	182.56	104	1868	F 1917
Centennial	Stern-Wheeler	559.50	155	1876	—1895
Ceres	Side-Wheeler	120.42	130.5	1876	—1899
Cherokee	Stern-Wheeler	740	179.2	1912	A 1939
Chesapeake	Propeller	...	...	—1850	—1868
Chin-Du-Wan	Side-Wheeler	181.54	155	1868	—1885
Christiana	Stern-Wheeler	...	...	1860	—1868
Chrysopolis[b]	Side-Wheeler	1,050	245	1860	{ R 1875 / F 1940
City of Dawson	Stern-Wheeler	230.93	114	1898	—1911
City of Stockton	Stern-Wheeler	823.70	175	1873	—1915
Clara	Stern-Wheeler	41	...	1854	—1868
Clara Bell	Stern-Wheeler	53.62	80.6	1871	—1885
Clara Crow	Stern-Wheeler	...	...	1848	—1885
Cleopatra	Stern-Wheeler	80	...	1853	—1872
Cochan[o] CR	Stern-Wheeler	234	135.5	1899	—1909
Cocopah (No. 1) CR	Stern-Wheeler	...	...	1858	D 1872
Cocopah (No. 2) CR	Stern-Wheeler	231.37	147.5	1867	D 1881
Colorado (No. 1) CR	Stern-Wheeler	...	120	1855	D 1862
Colorado (No. 2) CR	Stern-Wheeler	178.59	127	1862	—1890
Colusa (No. 1)	Stern-Wheeler	149.67	129.7	1861	—1881
Colusa (No. 2)	Stern-Wheeler	795	177.5	1911	F 1932
Commodore Jones[d]		31	...	1849	—1868
Commodore Preble	Propeller	...	...	—1859	—1868
Confidence[e]	Side-Wheeler	639	...	EC 1848	—1872
Constance	Stern-Wheeler	...	...	....	A 1918
Cora	Stern-Wheeler	298	...	—1868	—1872
Cornelia	Side-Wheeler	382	165.5	1853	—1877
Crockett (ex-H. J. Corcoran)	Stern-Wheeler	893	221	1898	US 1943
D. E. Knight	Stern-Wheeler	199	131.5	1875	—1905
Daisy	Stern-Wheeler	43.19	80	1879	—1890
Daniel Moore	Stern-Wheeler	63	...	1852	—1868
Dashaway		106.15	126.2	1857	—1868
Dauntless[f]	Stern-Wheeler	612	174.5	1892	R 1938
Delta King (steel)	Stern-Wheeler	1,837	250	1926	US 1942
Delta Queen (steel)	Stern-Wheeler	1,837	250	1926	US 1942
Dolphin	Side-Wheeler	...	...	1850	—1868
Dover (No. 1)	Stern-Wheeler	183.64	130	1869	—1885
Dover (No. 2)	Stern-Wheeler	244	150	1891	B 1935

[a] Renamed *Port of Stockton*.　　　　[b] Rebuilt as ferry steamer *Oakland*.

[o] Rebuilt from the *Gila*.　　　　[d] Renamed *Jack Hays*.

[e] Rebuilt as ferry steamer *San Antonio*.

[f] Rebuilt as motor vessel *San Joaquin;* lengthened to 190.5 feet.

Name	Type	Tons	Length	When Built	Disposal and Date
Eclipse	Side-Wheeler	498	...	EC1854	B 1855
Edna		30	...	1850	—1868
Edward Everett Junior	Stern-Wheeler	50	56	1849	Sn 1849
El Dorado		153	...	1849	—1868
Elk (No. 1)................		24.28	41	1869	—1872
Elk (No. 2)	Stern-Wheeler	97	75	1915	D 1918
Ellen (No. 1)		47.60	78.5	1869	—1872
Ellen (No. 2)	Stern-Wheeler	57.70	65.5	1885	—1919
Emma	Stern-Wheeler	87.87	85.2	1870	—1895
Empire		149	...	1851	A 1863
Empire City	Stern-Wheeler	102.36	106	1869	—1899
Enterprise (No. 1)		99	...	1854	—1868
Enterprise (No. 2)	Stern-Wheeler	246	136	1868	—1895
Erastus Corning		86	...	1850	—1868
Esmeralda CR	Stern-Wheeler	...	...	1864	—1868
Explorer (iron) CR	Stern-Wheeler	...	...	1857	Str —1872
Express (No. 1)	Stern-Wheeler	105	...	1851	—1868
Express (No. 2)	Stern-Wheeler	74	92	1870	—1877
F. M. Smith	Stern-Wheeler	295	125	1895	F 1909
Fanny Ann	Propeller	88.2	110	1862	—1881
Fashion	Stern-Wheeler	87	...	1850	—1877
Fawn	Side-Wheeler	90	...	1848	E 1850
Fay No. 4	Stern-Wheeler	179	136.2	1912	F 1920
Fire Fly (iron)	Propeller	...	...	1850	—1868
Flora (No. 1)	Stern-Wheeler	224.7	...	—1877	—1885
Flora (No. 2)	Stern-Wheeler	141	141	1885	F 1932
Flora Temple		223.17	132.5	1860	—1881
Fort Bragg[g]	Stern-Wheeler	317	155	1899	R 1921
Fort Sutter	Stern-Wheeler	1,139	219.2	1912	US 1942
Frances	Stern-Wheeler	698.44	174	1905	A 1941
Free Trade	Stern-Wheeler	300	...	—1852	—1868
Fruto	Stern-Wheeler	429.12	175	1899	A 1925
Gabriel Winter	Stern-Wheeler	73	...	1851	—1868
Game Cock		24	...	1851	—1868
Gazelle	Stern-Wheeler	81	...	1852	—1868
Gem	Stern-Wheeler	235	...	—1865	—1881
General Jessup CR	Side-Wheeler	49	...	1854	E 1859
General Warren	Propeller	...	...	EC—1848	—1868
Georgiana	Side-Wheeler	30	...	1850	E 1855
Gila[h] CR	Stern-Wheeler	236.47	135.5	1872	R 1899
Gold (No. 1)	Stern-Wheeler	334	155	1883	F 1920
Gold (No. 2) (ex-Fort Bragg) }	Stern-Wheeler	317	155	1899	A 1940
Gold Hunter	Propeller	435	...	EC—1850	—1868
Goliah	Side-Wheeler	235	154.5	EC1849	—1890
Goodman Castle	Stern-Wheeler	160.13	...	1850	—1885

[g] Rebuilt as the *Gold* (No. 2).   [h] Rebuilt as the *Cochan*.

Name	Type	Tons	Length	When Built	Disposal and Date
Governor Dana ....Stern-Wheeler		364.5	140	EC—1850	—1885
Grace Barton ....Stern-Wheeler		194.84	100	1890	F 1916
Guadalupe		...	...	—1859	—1868
Gypsy ....Propeller		293	102	1868	—1907
H. E. Wright ....Stern-Wheeler		562	168	1899	A 1928
H. J. Corcoran[i] ....Stern-Wheeler		682	209.5	1898	C 1913 R 1914
H. T. Clay ....Side-Wheeler		154	...	1850	—1868
Hartford ....Propeller		251	...	EC—1850	—1868
Harriett ....Stern-Wheeler		93.55	...	1869	—1877
Hattie Fickett ....Stern-Wheeler		332.55	151	1872	—1887
Helen Hensley ....Side-Wheeler		394.81	168.5	1853	A 1883
Herald ....Stern-Wheeler		147.83	127.5	1878	—1905
Hercules (No. 1) (naphtha) Stern-Wheeler		...	65	1903	D 1905
Hercules (No. 2) ....Stern-Wheeler		437	158.5	1907	—1920
Hope ....Stern-Wheeler		74.15	86	1870	—1885
Ion		...	30	1850	—1868
Isleton[j] ....Stern-Wheeler		615	167.5	1902	US 1942
J. A. McClelland		73.31	...	—1861	—1877
J. D. Peters ....Stern-Wheeler		880.7	206.5	1889	A 1938
J. R. McDonald ....Stern-Wheeler		137.56	104.5	1899	A 1918
Jacinto ....Stern-Wheeler		235	145	1889	F 1932
Jack Hayes (ex-R. K. Page)............		69	...	1852	—1868
Jack Hays (ex-Commodore Jones).......		31	...	1849	—1868
James Blair ....Stern-Wheeler		...	...	—1859	—1868
Jenny Lind ....Side-Wheeler		61	...	1850	E 1853
John A. Sutter		...	...	1849	E 1850
John Bragdon ....Side-Wheeler		273	150	EC1851	A 1865
Josie McNear ....Side-Wheeler		136.72	108.7	1865	—1881
Julia ....Side-Wheeler		503	170	1870	E 1888
Kangaroo ....Stern-Wheeler		...	...	—1859	—1868
Kate Kearny		112	...	1851	A 1859
Kennebec ....Stern-Wheeler		44	...	1850	—1868
Knight No. 2 ....Stern-Wheeler		247.8	137	1885	—1905
Lady Washington[k] ......Stern-Wheeler		...	...	1849	—1868
Latona ....Stern-Wheeler		...	...	—1859	—1868
Lawrence		...	108	1849	—1868
Leader ....Stern-Wheeler		304	144	1884	D 1938
Linda		52	...	1849	—1868
Major Tompkins ....Propeller		...	...	EC—1850	—1868
Mariposa ....Side-Wheeler		60	...	1850	—1868
Maria ....Stern-Wheeler		...	...	—1859	—1868
Martha Jane ....Stern-Wheeler		...	...	—1850	—1868
Martin White ....Side-Wheeler		189	...	1854	—1877
Mary B. Williams[l] ....Stern-Wheeler		137.98	98.6	1877	—1917

[i] Rebuilt as the *Crockett.*
[j] Rebuilt as motor vessel; later sold to United States Army and renamed the *Army Queen.*
[k] Renamed *Ohio.*   [l] Renamed *Victory.*

Name	Type	Tons	Length	When Built	Disposal and Date
Mary Ellen	...	...	...	—1862	—1868
Mary Garrett ....Stern-Wheeler	810.28	172	1878	—1915
Marysville ....Stern-Wheeler	51	...	1851	—1868
Maunsel White (iron) ......Side-Wheeler	36	...	1850	—1868
McKim ....Propeller	400	...	EC—1849	—1868
Medea ....Stern-Wheeler	25	...	1853	—1868
Merrimac ....Propeller	48.51	...	—1866	—1877
Miner	75	...	1850	—1868
Mint (iron)	36	...	1849	—1868
Missouri	27	...	1850	—1868
Modoc ....Stern-Wheeler	929	207	1880	A 1928
Mohave (No. 1) CR .....Stern-Wheeler	192.61	133	1866	D 1874
Mohave (No. 2) CR .....Stern-Wheeler	188.03	149.5	1876	—1901
Monarch ....Stern-Wheeler	195.47	109	1875	—1911
Moulton ....Stern-Wheeler	192.76	150.5	1867	—1881
Mount Eden ....Stern-Wheeler	73.66	89.5	1875	—1910
Napa City ....Stern-Wheeler	178.87	106	1891	A 1931
Navajo ....Stern-Wheeler	1,122	252	1909	A 1938
Neponset No. 2 ....Stern-Wheeler	224	125.1	1884	Sn 1921
Nevada ....Side-Wheeler	...	...	1861	Sn 1863
New England (iron)	28	50	1849	—1868
New Orleans ....Stern-Wheeler	...	...	—1850	—1868
Newton ....Stern-Wheeler	77	75	1901	B 1904
Newton No. 2 ....Stern-Wheeler	217.18	131.5	1905	A 1926
New World ....Side-Wheeeler	530	...	EC1850	B 1879
Nina Tilden CR ....Stern-Wheeler	107.4	98	—1872	—1885
O.K.	78.35	...	—1862	—1881
Ohio (ex-*Lady Washington*) Stern-Wheeler	...	...	1849	—1868
Onisbo ....Stern-Wheeler	632	178.1	1900	A 1923
Onward ....Stern-Wheeler	388.8	165	1877	—1909
Orient ....Stern-Wheeler	...	...	1850	—1868
Oriole ....Stern-Wheeler	68.10	81.5	1905	F 1921
Parthenius ....Side-Wheeler	294	154	1869	—1881
Paul Pry ....Side-Wheeler	330	...	—1859	—1881
Pearl	78	...	1854	E 1855
Pert	...	...	—1862	—1868
Petaluma (No. 1)	365	...	1857	—1900
Petaluma (No. 2) (ex-*Resolute*) ......Stern-Wheeler	264	134.2	1884	F 1914
Petaluma (No. 3) ....Stern-Wheeler	448	148.4	1914	....
Peytona	...	...	—1859	—1868
Pike (ex-*Rip*) ....Stern-Wheeler	...	153	1852	—1868
Pilot	145	...	1865	—1885
Pioneer (No. 1) ....Side-Wheeler	80	...	1849	Sn 1849
Pioneer (No. 2) ....Stern-Wheeler	137.27	100.5	1867	—1877
Plumas ....Stern-Wheeler	51	...	1853	Sn 1854
Potrero ....Stern-Wheeler	531	145	1900	....

Name	Type	Tons	Length	When Built	Disposal and Date
Port of Stockton (ex-*Capital City*)	Stern-Wheeler	1,142	220	1910	US 1942
Pride of the River	Stern-Wheeler	619.15	175	1878	A 1942
R. K. Page[m]		69	...	1852	—1868
Rambler	Side-Wheeler	...	...	—1857	—1868
Ranger		30	...	1853	E 1854
Redding	Stern-Wheeler	...	...	—1850	—1868
Red Bluff (No. 1)		243.66	...	—1868	Fo 1880
Red Bluff (No. 2)	Stern-Wheeler	246.17	150.6	1884	—1890
Red Bluff (No. 3)	Stern-Wheeler	246	150	1894	B 1936
Red Jacket		...	...	—1850	—1868
Reform (No. 1)	Stern-Wheeler	181	...	—1877	—1885
Reform (No. 2)	Stern-Wheeler	627.69	...	1898	A 1938
Relief	Stern-Wheeler	145	99	1864	—1895
Resolute[n]	Stern-Wheeler	264	134.2	1884	F 1914
Rip[o]	Stern-Wheeler	153	...	1852	—1868
S. B. Wheeler	Stern-Wheeler	120	...	EC1849	SA 1854
S. W. Whipple	Stern-Wheeler	292.01	173	1877	—1881
Sacramento (No. 1)	Side-Wheeler	...	60	1849	—1868
Sacramento (No. 2)	Side-Wheeler	540.8	171.5	1861	—1872
Sacramento (No. 3)		60.22	75	1869	—1877
Sacramento (No. 4)	Stern-Wheeler	760	178	1914	F 1932
Sagamore		66	...	1850	E 1850
St. Vallier (steel) CR	Stern-Wheeler	92	74.3	1899	—1909
Samuel Soule	Stern-Wheeler	87	...	1855	—1868
San Joaquin	Side-Wheeler	77.6	...	1860	—1881
San Joaquin No. 2	Stern-Wheeler	242.77	145	1875	F 1932
San Joaquin No. 3	Stern-Wheeler	220.95	145	1877	F 1910
San Joaquin No. 4	Stern-Wheeler	365.43	163	1885	F 1932
San Jose	Stern-Wheeler	192	101	1898	F 1932
San Lorenzo	Stern-Wheeler	72.01	89	1874	—1885
Santa Clara		...	...	1851	F 1851
Sarah		...	...	EC1850	—1868
Satellite		...	...	—1860	—1868
Sea Bird		...	...	—1850	—1868
Sea Gull	Stern-Wheeler	44.73	84.5	1899	B 1912
Searchlight CR	Stern-Wheeler	98	91.2	1903	—1909
Secretary		...	...	—1854	E 1854
Seizer (snag boat)	Stern-Wheeler	...	157	1881	D 1921
Seminole	Stern-Wheeler	1,102.48	220	1911	C 1913
Senator	Side-Wheeler	750	226	EC1848	D 1882
Sentinel	Stern-Wheeler	99	90.1	1908	F 1919
Shasta	Stern-Wheeler	120	110	1853	—1868
Sitka[p]	Side-Wheeler	40	37	1847	R 1848

[m] Renamed *Jack Hayes*.   [n] Renamed *Petaluma* (No. 2).

[o] Renamed *Pike*.

[p] First California river steamboat; rebuilt as schooner *Rainbow*.

Name	Type	Tons	Length	When Built	Disposal and Date
Solano	Stern-Wheeler	146.88	109.5	1866	—1885
Sonoma	Stern-Wheeler	197.03	109	1874	A 1915
Sophie	Side-Wheeler	148	...	1851	—1868
Sophie McLane		...	...	—1859	E 1864
Star		22	...	EC1850	—1868
Stockton	Stern-Wheeler	...	...	—1853	—1868
Surprise	Side-Wheeler	...	...	EC1855	SA —1868
Swan	Stern-Wheeler	...	...	—1859	—1868
T. C. Walker (No. 1)		256	...	—1868	—1881
T. C. Walker (No. 2)	Stern-Wheeler	786.9	200	1885	A 1938
Tehama	Stern-Wheeler	83	...	1850	—1885
Telephone	Stern-Wheeler	632	201	1903	—1918
Thomas Hunt	Side-Wheeler	370	...	EC1851	SA 1855
Tiger	Stern-Wheeler	85.37	...	1875	D 1916
Tulare	Stern-Wheeler	166.02	111.8	1867	—1885
Tuolumne City	Stern-Wheeler	...	90	1868	—1885
Underwriter	Side-Wheeler	433	...	EC1854	F 1857
Uncle Sam CR	Side-Wheeler	...	65	1851	Fo 1854
Union (iron)	Side-Wheeler	87	...	1850	—1877
Urilda	Side-Wheeler	140	...	EC1851	A 1858
Valletta	Stern-Wheeler	419	176	1901	F 1932
Vaquero	Stern-Wheeler	105.92	100	1865	—1885
Varuna (No. 1)	Stern-Wheeler	216.10	141	1873	—1895
Varuna (No. 2)	Stern-Wheeler	230	143	1895	—1907
Victor Constant	Stern-Wheeler	57	...	1850	—1868
Victory (ex-*Mary B. Williams*)	Stern-Wheeler	137.98	98.6	1877	—1917
Visalia		135.88	...	—1860	—1881
Washington	Stern-Wheeler	148.58	99.7	1866	—1877
Washoe	Side-Wheeler	580	...	1864	B 1878
Weitchpec	Stern-Wheeler	150	100.9	1904	F 1920
West Point	Side-Wheeler	...	...	EC—1850	—1868
Willamette	Side-Wheeeler	...	...	—1852	—1868
William Robinson	Side-Wheeler	...	...	—1850	—1868
Wilson G. Hunt	Side-Wheeler	450	185.5	EC1849	B 1890
Yosemite	Side-Wheeler	1,319	283	1862	Str 1909
Young America		67	...	1854	—1868
Yuba	Stern-Wheeler	...	...	—1850	—1868
Yuba (snag boat)	Stern-Wheeler	...	166	1925	....
Yuba City Belle	Stern-Wheeler	31.9	74	1875	—1885
Zinfandel	Stern-Wheeler	329	125	1889	Fo 1922

CALIFORNIA STEAMBOAT BUILDERS

In few cases has any record been preserved of the shipyard in which individual vessels were built, and those which produced the earlier steamers have long since gone out of business. While far from complete, the list given herewith shows those builders whose names—all too often merely the surnames—could be established as definitely connected with the particular vessels listed. The list, so far as it goes, is as follows:

Bissett & Delaney, Stockton: *Mary B. Williams*

Ralph Butler, San Francisco: *Orient*

California Transportation Company, Stockton: *Delta King, Delta Queen* (hulls prefabricated in Scotland)

William E. Collyer, San Francisco: *James M. Donahue;* several ferries

Cousins, Stockton: *S. W. Whipple, Josie McNear, Moulton*

George D. Damon, Oakland: *Onward, Pride of the River*

Stephen Davis, Stockton: *Centennial, Chin-Du-Wan, City of Stockton, Clara Bell, Cora, Empire City, Enterprise, Harriett, Herald, Relief, T. C. Walker, Tulare, Tuolumne City*

Delaney, Benicia: *Valletta*

Dickie Brothers, San Francisco: *Tiger, San Lorenzo*

Gates, Sacramento: *Bullion*

John Haggerty, San Francisco: *Fanny Ann*

Haight, Soquel: *Pioneer* (No. 2)

Samuel J. Hensley, Stockton: *Helen Hensley*

Keeps & Bergen, Stockton: *Ellen, Emma*

Littleton & Company, San Francisco: *Shasta, Plumas*

Marcucci, Stockton: *Brisk, Mary Garratt*

Middlemas, Oakland: *Solano*

Middlemas & Boole, San Francisco: *Gipsy, Governor Stanford*

John G. North, San Francisco: *Capital, Chrysopolis, Contra Costa, Parthenius, Reform* (No. 1); several ferries

Nuttson, Vallejo: *Belle*

Orr, Yuba City: *Yuba City Belle*

Owens, San Francisco: *Amelia, Washoe;* also liner *Ancon*

James Robertson, San Francisco: *Capital City, Fort Sutter;* several ferries

James Robertson, Benicia: *Petaluma* (No. 3)

Sacramento Transportation Company, Broderick: *Dover* (No. 2), *Flora, Jacinto, Red Bluff* (No. 3), *San Joaquin No. 2, San Joaquin No. 3, San Joaquin No. 4, Varuna* (No. 2)

Schultz & Robertson, San Francisco: *Colusa, Sacramento* (No. 4)

C. Small, Stockton: *Mount Eden*

Southern Pacific Railway, Oakland: *Apache, Modoc, Navajo, Seminole;* numerous ferries

Patrick Tiernan, San Francisco: *Amador, Gila, Pilot, Red Bluff* (No. 1), *Sacramento* (No. 3); several ferries

Walton, San Francisco: *Rip*

C. M. Wylie, Union City: *Caroline*

That accounts for only seventy-two of them—roughly, about twenty-five per cent of the total number of vessels which plied the rivers. It is more than likely that the builders listed herein launched other river steamers, and it is certain that there were many other builders whose names are not shown. Some were regular shipwrights, and some were merely the future owners themselves, assisted by such ship-carpenters as they could gather together at some level spot along the shores of river or bay. These worthy souls hardly could be expected to preserve building data for posterity; in many cases, it is said, the backer of the enterprise would start out by taking a sharp stick and drawing an outline on the ground—

"Now, boys," he'd say, "we're goin' to build a steamboat . . . . about this size . . . ."

APPENDIX C

TABLE OF DISTANCES,* RIVER LANDINGS

	Miles	Elevation
San Francisco to Benicia	30	
San Francisco to Collinsville	75	
San Francisco to Rio Vista	80	
San Francisco to Sacramento	125	30 feet
Sacramento to Russian Crossing	12	
Sacramento to Fremont	26	
Sacramento to Marysville (Feather River)	41	72 feet
Sacramento to Knight's Landing	46	
Sacramento to Eagle Bend	54	
Sacramento to Three Rivers	64	
Sacramento to Poker Bend	69	
Sacramento to George Howell's	74	
Sacramento to Big Eddy	79	
Sacramento to Dry Slough	87	
Sacramento to Eddy's	95	
Sacramento to Twenty-Mile Island	105	
Sacramento to Font's Ferry	112	
Sacramento to Butte Creek	118	
Sacramento to Colusa	125	177 feet
Sacramento to Sherman's	132	
Sacramento to Snyder's	136	
Sacramento to Nine-Mile House	141	
Sacramento to Boggs	146	
Sacramento to Princeton	151	
Sacramento to Butte City	158	
Sacramento to Cut-Off	165	
Sacramento to Pike's	170	
Sacramento to Plaza City	179	
Sacramento to Jennings'	188	
Sacramento to Monroeville	191	
Sacramento to Chico	199	190 feet
Sacramento to Bidwell's	205	
Sacramento to Sam Soule's Landing	212	
Sacramento to Gazelle Shoot	225	
Sacramento to Moon's	232	
Sacramento to Mahew's	240	

* Distances are in statute miles, and in the case of the Sacramento and San Joaquin rivers are from steamboat schedules published before the days of such distance-saving projects as the straightening out of Horseshoe Bend on the Sacramento or the dredging of Venice Cut, Mandeville Cut, and similar tangents through the San Joaquin Delta. For the Colorado River the distances were estimated from charts and maps, no two published authorities having been found to agree on any of them.

	Miles	Elevation
Sacramento to Squaw House	245	
Sacramento to Tehama	248	
Sacramento to Red Bluff	270	304 feet
San Francisco to Red Bluff	395	

SAN JOAQUIN RIVER

	Miles	Elevation
San Francisco to New York Slough	45	
San Francisco to Antioch	50	
San Francisco to Mokelumne River	67	
San Francisco to Stockton	127	19 feet
Stockton to Shepard's	21	
Stockton to Allison's	41	
Stockton to Dunham's Ferry	51	
Stockton to San Joaquin	54	
Stockton to South Tuolumne	64	
Stockton to Graysonville	74	
Stockton to Bell's	82	
Stockton to Patterson's	91	
Stockton to Ward's	93	
Stockton to Crow's	100	115 feet
Stockton to Hill's Ferry	111	
Stockton to South Merced	115	
Stockton to Dover	140	
Stockton to Johnson's Landing.............	180	
Stockton to Coopertown	186	
Stockton to Miller's Landing	196	
Stockton to Temple's Landing	202	
Stockton to Firebaugh's Ferry	217	156 feet
Stockton to Aliso	232	
Stockton to Watson's Ferry	248	
Stockton to Sycamore Point	272	
San Francisco to Sycamore Point	399	

COLORADO RIVER

	Miles	Elevation
Port Isabel to Yuma	122	139 feet
Port Isabel to Castle Dome	157	
Port Isabel to Ehrenberg	214	
Port Isabel to Aubry	232	
Port Isabel to Camp Mohave	304	540 feet
Port Isabel to Hardyville	312	
Port Isabel to El Dorado Canyon	354	
Port Isabel to Callville	380	945 feet

CALIFORNIA FERRY VESSELS

Key to Symbols: A, abandoned; C, lost by collision; D, dismantled; DD, Diesel (direct) drive; DE, Diesel (electric) drive; F, lost by fire; HB, Humboldt Bay ferry; LA, Los Angeles Harbor ferry; R, rebuilt; SA, sold to aliens; SD, San Diego Bay ferry; SE, single-ender; TE, turbine-electric drive; US, transferred to United States government. The minus sign before the date indicates vessel not in the record prior to that year. All vessels steam-powered and of wooden construction unless otherwise noted.

Name and Place of Operation	Type	Gross Tons	Length	When Built	Disposal and Date
Ada HB	Stern-Wheeler	64	71	1874	—1907
Alameda (No. 1)	Side-Wheeler	813	193	1866	D 1898
Alameda (No. 2) (steel)	Side-Wheeler	2,302	293	1913	....
Alta HB	Stern-Wheeler	64	71	1874	—1907
Annie HB	Stern-Wheeler	83	76	1883	—1902
Antelope (No. 1) HB	Stern-Wheeler	155	95	1888	D 1909
Antelope (No. 2) HB	Stern-Wheeler	160	100	1910	....
Argo HB	Stern-Wheeler	44	54	1898	—1900
Asbury Park (steel)	SE Propeller	3,016	297	1903	....
Bay City	Side-Wheeler	1,283	247	1878	D 1930
Benicia SD	Side-Wheeler	144	92	1881	D 1904
Berkeley (steel)	Propeller	1,945	279	1898	....
Calistoga (steel)	SE Propeller	2,280	298	1907	US 1942
Cazadero	Side-Wheeler	1,682	228	1903	US 1943
City of Sacramento (ex-*Asbury Park*)	...	...	...	....	....
City of San Rafael (steel)	Side-Wheeler	484	172	1924	....
Claremont	Propeller	1,138	189	1907	—1928
Clinton		194	...	1853	C 1881
Contra Costa (No. 1)	SE Side-Wheeler	449	170	1857	—1885
Contra Costa (No. 2)	Side-Wheeler	5,373	433	1914	D 1934
Coronado (No. 1) SD	Side-Wheeler	308	100	1886	A 1922
Coronado (No. 2) (steel) SD	DE Propeller	502	178	1929	....
Diana	Propeller	...	100	—1868	—1885
Edward T. Jeffrey (ex-*Feather River*)	...	...	...	....	....
El Capitan	Side-Wheeler	982	194	1868	D 1925
El Paso (steel)	Propeller	929	234	1924	....
Elwha (ex-*Golden Shore*)		...	...	....	....
Encinal	Side-Wheeler	2,014	274	1888	D 1930
Eureka (ex-*Ukiah*)		...	...	....	....
Feather River (steel)	Propeller	1,578	218	1913	....
Fernwood	Propeller	1,160	194	1907	A 1938
Fresno (steel)	Propeller	1,024	251	1927	....
Garden City	Side-Wheeler	1,080	243	1897	D 1930

Name and Place of Operation	Type	Gross Tons	Length	When Built	Disposal and Date
General Frisbie	SE Propeller	670	187	1900	....
Glide	Stern-Wheeler	...	...	1854	—1882
Golden Age	DE Propeller	779	226	1928	A 1938
Golden Bear	DE Propeller	779	226	1927	—1939
Golden Coast (ex-*Yerba Buena* No. 1) ...		...	...	....	....
Golden Dawn (ex-*San Francisco*)		...	...	....	....
Golden Era (ex-*Fernwood*)		...	...	....	....
Golden Gate	DE Propeller	598	206	1922	A 1937
Golden Poppy	DE Propeller	779	226	1927	—1938
Golden Shore	DE Propeller	779	226	1927	—1939
Golden State	DE Propeller	780	226	1926	—1939
Golden West	DE Propeller	594	214	1923	R 1938
Hayward	TE Propeller	1,653	225	1923	....
Illahee (ex-*Lake Tahoe*)		...	...	....	....
Islander LA	DD Propeller	283	119	1916	....
James M. Donahue	SE Side-Wheeler	730	219	1874	D 1924
Kalakala (ex-*Peralta*)	DD Propeller	1,417	225	R 1935	....
Kehloken (ex-*Golden State*)		...	...	....	....
Klamath (steel)	Propeller	1,025	251	1927	....
Klickitat (ex-*Stockton*)		...	...	....	....
Lagunitas	Stern-Wheeler	767	250	1903	A 1922
Lake Tahoe (steel)	DE Propeller	1,025	251	1927	....
Malahat (ex-*Napa Valley*)		...	...	....	....
Marin (ex-*Requa*)		...	..	....	....
Melrose	Side-Wheeler	2,662	294	1908	D 1931
Mendocino (steel)	DE Propeller	1,026	251	1927	....
Milton S. Latham	Stern-Wheeler	263	160	1860	—1888
Morena SD	Side-Wheeler	381	156	1920	US 1942
Napa Valley (steel)	SE Propeller	2,189	231	1910	....
New Orleans (steel)	Propeller	1,952	234	1924	....
Newark	Side-Wheeler	1,783	276	1877	R 1923
Nisqually (ex-*Mendocino*)		...	...	....	....
North Island (ex-*Golden West*) SD		...	...	....	....
Oakland (No. 1)	Side-Wheeler	285	...	1858	D 1874
Oakland (No. 2) (ex-*Chrysopolis*) }	Side-Wheeler	1,672	283	1875	F 1940
Oneatta HB	Stern-Wheeler	118	82	1872	—1889
Peralta (steel)	TE Propeller	2,075	255	1927	R 1935
Petaluma of Sausalito ...	SE Side-Wheeler	365	150	1857	—1900
Piedmont	Side-Wheeler	1,854	273	1883	D 1938
Princess	SE Side-Wheeler	193	...	—1859	—1881
Quinault (ex-*Redwood Empire*)		...	...	....	....
Ramona SD	Side-Wheeler	417	118	1903	D 1932
Redwood Empire (steel) ...	DE Propeller	1,025	251	1927	....
Requa	SE Side-Wheeler	101	88	1909	....
Russian River (ex-*New Orleans*)		...	...	....	....
Sacramento (No. 1)		...	...	1869	—1885

Name and Place of Operation	Type	Gross Tons	Length	When Built	Disposal and Date
Sacramento (No. 2) (ex-*Newark*)	Side-Wheeler	2,197	295	R 1923	....
San Antonio (ex-*Confidence*)	Side-Wheeler	639	...	1848	—1872
San Diego (steel) SD	DE Propeller	556	192	1931	....
San Francisco	Propeller	612	180	1905	D 1939
San Jose	Propeller	1,115	175	1903	R 1919
San Leandro (steel)	TE Propeller	1,653	225	1923	....
San Mateo (steel)	Propeller	1,782	216	1927	....
San Pablo	Side-Wheeler	1,584	226	1900	A 1938
San Pedro (steel)	Side-Wheeler	1,720	248	1911	....
San Rafael	SE Side-Wheeler	692	205	1877	C 1901
Santa Clara (steel)	Side-Wheeler	2,282	293	1914	....
Saucelito	SE Side-Wheeler	692	205	1878	F 1883
Sausalito	Side-Wheeler	1,766	236	1894	—1935
Sierra Nevada (ex-*Edward T. Jeffrey*)	...	...	...	....	....
Silver Gate	Propeller	528	187	1888	D 1902[*]
Silver Strand (ex-*Elwha*) SD	...	...	...	....	....
Solano	Side-Wheeler	3,549	420	1879	D 1934
Sonoma Valley (ex-*San Jose*)	...	...	...	....	....
Stockton (steel)	DE Propeller	1,028	251	1927	....
Tamalpais (No. 1) (ex-*Petaluma of Sausalito*)	...	...	...	....	....
Tamalpais (No. 2)	Side-Wheeler	1,631	224	1901	US 1943
Thoroughfare (No. 1)	Side-Wheeler	1,012	248	1871	D 1909
Thoroughfare (No. 2)	Side-Wheeler	2,605	294	1912	D 1935
Tiburon	Side-Wheeler	1,248	220	1881	D 1925
Transit	Side-Wheeler	1,566	338	1876	D 1934
Treasure Island (ex-*San Pedro*)	...	...	...	....	....
Treasure Island (ex-*Marin*)	DD Propeller	...	...	....	....
Ukiah	Side-Wheeler	2,420	277	1890	....
Yerba Buena (No. 1)	Propeller	1,115	175	1903	A 1938
Yerba Buena (No. 2) (steel)	TE Propeller	2,075	256	1927	....
Yosemite (steel)	Propeller	1,782	216	1923	SA 1940

[*] Date document surrendered. Actually out of service in 1888.

APPENDIX E

CHANGES OF NAME, FERRY VESSELS

Original Name	Subsequent Name and Place of Transfer
Asbury Park	*City of Sacramento*
Feather River	*Edward T. Jeffrey, Sierra Nevada*
Fernwood	*Golden Era*
Fresno	*Willapa* (Puget Sound)
General Frisbie	*Commander* (fishing vessel)
Golden Age	*Klahanie* (Puget Sound)
Golden Poppy	*Chetzmoka* (Puget Sound)
Golden Shore	*Elwha* (Puget Sound), *Silver Strand* (San Diego)
Golden State	*Kehloken* (Puget Sound)
Golden West	*North Island* (San Diego)
Lake Tahoe	*Illahee* (Puget Sound)
Mendocino	*Nisqually* (Puget Sound)
Newark	*Sacramento*
New Orleans	*Russian River*
Peralta	*Kalakala* (Puget Sound)
Petaluma of Sausalito	*Tamalpais* (No. 1)
Redwood Empire	*Quinault* (Puget Sound)
Requa	*Marin, Treasure Island*
San Francisco	*Golden Dawn*
San Jose	*Sonoma Valley*
San Pedro	*Treasure Island*
Stockton	*Klickitat* (Puget Sound)
Ukiah	*Eureka*
Yerba Buena (No. 1)	*Golden Coast*
Yosemite	*Argentina* (Montevideo)

INDEX